THE GLOBAL THREAT OF
TERRORISM

By Jason Brainard

Portions of this book originally appeared in *Terrorism* by Debra A. Miller.

LUCENT PRESS

Published in 2020 by
Lucent Press, an Imprint of Greenhaven Publishing, LLC
353 3rd Avenue
Suite 255
New York, NY 10010

Designer: Deanna Paternostro
Editor: Jennifer Lombardo

Library of Congress Cataloging-in-Publication Data

Names: Brainard, Jason, author.
Title: The global threat of terrorism / Jason Brainard.
Description: First Edition. | New York : Lucent Press, [2020] | Series: Hot
    topics | Includes bibliographical references and index.
Identifiers: LCCN 2018048629 (print) | LCCN 2018050964 (ebook) | ISBN
    9781534567580 (eBook) | ISBN 9781534567573 (pbk. book) | ISBN
    9781534566965 (library bound book)
Subjects: LCSH: Terrorism–History.
Classification: LCC HV6431 (ebook) | LCC HV6431 .B7343 2020 (print) | DDC
    363.325–dc23
LC record available at https://lccn.loc.gov/2018048629

Printed in the United States of America

CPSIA compliance information: Batch #BS19KL: For further information contact Greenhaven Publishing LLC, New York,
New York at 1-844-317-7404.

Please visit our website, www.greenhavenpublishing.com. For a free color catalog of all our
high-quality books, call toll free 1-844-317-7404 or fax 1-844-317-7405.

CONTENTS

Adolescence is a time when many people begin to take notice of the world around them. News channels, blogs, and talk radio shows are constantly promoting one view or another; very few are unbiased. Young people also hear conflicting information from parents, friends, teachers, and acquaintances. Often, they will hear only one side of an issue or be given flawed information. People who are trying to support a particular viewpoint may cite inaccurate facts and statistics on their blogs, and news programs present many conflicting views of important issues in our society. In a world where it seems everyone has a platform to share their thoughts, it can be difficult to find unbiased, accurate information about important issues.

It is not only facts that are important. In blog posts, in comments on online videos, and on talk shows, people will share opinions that are not necessarily true or false but can still have a strong impact. For example, many young people struggle with their body image. Seeing or hearing negative comments about particular body types online can have a huge effect on the way someone views himself or herself and may lead to depression and anxiety. Although it is important not to keep information hidden from young people under the guise of protecting them, it is equally important to offer encouragement on issues that affect their mental health.

The titles in the Hot Topics series provide readers with different viewpoints on important issues in today's society. Many of these issues, such as gang violence and gun control laws, are of immediate concern to young people. This series aims to give readers factual context on these crucial topics in a way that lets them form their own opinions. The facts presented throughout also serve to empower readers to help themselves or support people they know who are struggling with many of the challenges adolescents face today. Although negative viewpoints are not ignored or downplayed, this series allows young people to see that the challenges they face are not insurmountable. As increasing numbers of young adults join political debates, especially regarding gun violence, learning the facts as well as the views of others will help them decide where they stand—and understand what they are fighting for.

Quotes encompassing all viewpoints are presented and cited so readers can trace them back to their original source, verifying for themselves whether the information comes from a reputable place. Additional books and websites are listed, giving readers a starting point from which to continue their own research. Chapter questions encourage discussion, allowing young people to hear and understand their classmates' points of view as they further solidify their own. Full-color photographs and enlightening charts provide a deeper understanding of the topics at hand. All of these features augment the informative text, helping young people understand the world they live in and formulate their own opinions concerning the best way they can improve it.

A New Kind of War

In 1991, the Soviet Union—which was made up of what is now Russia and other parts of Eastern Europe—collapsed due to internal economic and political problems. The Cold War that had been waged between the United States and the Soviet Union since the 1940s was over, and the threat of a direct Soviet military attack on the United States seemingly disappeared overnight. The democracy Americans championed had outlived the Communism of the Soviets. American policy makers and citizens alike breathed sighs of relief and allowed the threat of an attack on their way of life to fade into the back of their minds because they believed there would be no Soviet nuclear attack on U.S. soil. However, this newfound sense of well-being lasted only a decade. On September 11, 2001, terrorist attacks on the United States changed not only the nation, but also the rest of the world. President George W. Bush declared a war on terror, giving new focus to the nation's foreign and domestic policies.

During the Cold War, U.S. national security policy was centered on maintaining military superiority over the Soviet Union and limiting Soviet influence around the world. Over the course of more than four decades, this cost American taxpayers hundreds of billions of dollars in defense spending and aid to other nations that promised to oppose the Communism of the Soviet Union. Like the Cold War, the war on terrorism came with huge costs. Not only were trillions of dollars spent on wars in Afghanistan and Iraq, but thousands of United States soldiers were also killed. Countless others were wounded. Hundreds of thousands of civilians were killed in Iraq, Afghanistan, and neighboring Pakistan.

In 2006, in a speech at the U.S. military academy at West Point, Bush compared the war on terrorism to the Cold War and promised that the United States would show the same dedication to fighting terrorists that it did against the Soviets. Bush stated,

> Like the Cold War, our enemies believe that the innocent can be murdered to serve a political vision ... Like the Cold War, they're seeking weapons of mass murder that will allow them to deliver catastrophic destruction to our country ... If our enemies succeed in acquiring such weapons, they will not hesitate to use them, which means they would pose a threat to America as great as the Soviet Union.[1]

The terrorist enemies President Bush referred to were known as jihadists—Islamist extremists who wanted the United States to leave the Middle East so that Islamist rule could be instituted throughout the region. The initial terrorist threat to the United States was al-Qaeda—the group that claimed responsibility for the September 11 attacks and previous terrorist attacks against the United States. Although al-Qaeda has arguably not carried out another successful attack within the United States since September 11, 2001—more frequently called 9/11—it grew into a global terrorist network that gave rise to other terrorist organizations that have continued to attack countless targets, including U.S. soldiers and military barracks as well as civilian tourist sites frequently visited by Americans. Since 2001, groups with connections to al-Qaeda have mounted successful suicide attacks in places such as Indonesia, Kenya, Pakistan, Morocco, Turkey, Saudi Arabia, Spain, Great Britain, Jordan, and Iraq. Since the U.S. invasion of Iraq in 2003, Iraqi fighters associated with al-Qaeda have conducted unrelenting attacks against U.S. forces and Iraqi civilians. In addition, new Islamist terrorist groups have formed and grown to rival al-Qaeda in size and ferocity. The most notable offshoot of al-Qaeda has been the Islamic State in Iraq and the Levant (ISIL), also known as the Islamic State in Iraq and Syria (ISIS).

Understanding the Terms

Some terms referring to Islam, especially in reference to terrorism, tend to be used interchangeably by the general public. However, there are important differences between them. Below are the most commonly confused terms.

Islam: A religion centering around one god named Allah and his prophet Muhammad.

Islamic: Relating to Islam as it is taught by the majority of religious leaders—for example, "Islamic texts."

Islamism: Islamic extremism and fundamentalism; seeing Islam as a militant philosophy, in contrast with most mainstream teachings, which advocate peace.

Islamist: A person who believes in Islamism. Some of these extremists falsely call themselves Muslims.

Muslim: A person who practices mainstream Islam and rejects Islamism.

The development of new communication technologies—including the internet—and weapons has increased terrorists' capabilities. Some people have been convinced to join radical terrorist groups by viewing sophisticated propaganda that bombards them with violent messages, images, and tactics. The spread of weapons of mass destruction (WMDs)—including biological, chemical, or nuclear weapons—is also a huge concern. Terrorist groups are known to be interested in acquiring such weapons, and many experts predict that the result could be catastrophic suicide attacks in the future. Many experts expect terrorism to continue to spread. They believe these threats require a counterterrorism effort equal to the U.S. Cold War offensive.

Many other commentators, however, downplay the significance of the terrorist threat and say it should not define American foreign policy the way the Cold War did. Critics argue that terrorism is a tactic, not an ideology like Communism, and declaring war against a tactic makes no sense. In addition, commentators note that terrorism, unlike the Cold War, does not involve a conflict with another nation or group of nations that pose a military threat to the United States. Terrorism, these critics say, is simply a type of sensational violence used by relatively weak extremist groups to attract media publicity and influence government policy—essentially a nonmilitary threat designed to inspire fear in people they perceive as their enemies. In fact, experts say terrorism does not pose a serious physical risk to most Americans; the chances of being harmed by a terrorist attack within the United States, now or in the future, are very low. This means terrorists may not be an enemy worthy of a total commitment of the nation's military forces and energies. As retired diplomat Ronald Spiers put it, "Relying principally on military means [to fight terrorism] is like trying to eliminate a cloud of mosquitoes with a machine gun."[2] Moreover, many observers think that exaggerating the terrorist threat will increase public fears, which in turn may actually aid the terrorists' cause.

Whether the war on terror will continue to be pursued with the same means and priority as the Cold War struggle may depend on a number of factors. Another high-casualty terrorist attack in the United States could increase public fears and help maintain the war on terror. However, since the Great Recession—a period of economic decline from December 2007 to June 2009, from which many people and businesses are still recovering even in 2019—many Americans appear less concerned with international terrorism and more concerned with issues such as the country's economy and immigration policies. In fact, it is argued that homegrown terrorist organizations advocating white supremacy—the belief that white people are superior to all other races, frequently accompanied by violence against people of color—combined with an extreme form of nationalism are a greater, more rapidly growing threat to U.S. citizens than distant, foreign-based organizations.

CHAPTER 1

Terrorism as a Concept

A universal definition of terrorism is hard to pin down. Academics, diplomats, military experts, and political leaders may all define it differently. The difficulty in defining the concept of terrorism lies in the fact that throughout history, there have been many different forms of violent struggle that have used terror as a tool. Acts of terror have included everything from revolution against government oppression to battles fought for land or independence to acts of genocide committed by reigning governments. By the early 2000s, religious fanaticism had inspired some terrorists to take a new turn toward massive acts of violence against innocent civilians and private property. All of these examples of

On September 11, 2001, terrorists hijacked airplanes and crashed them into the twin towers of the World Trade Center in New York City and the Pentagon near Washington, D.C. A fourth hijacked plane crashed in Pennsylvania.

violence have been classified as terrorism by experts at one time or another.

Terrorism Is Violent

American historian and well-known terrorism expert Walter Laqueur has counted more than 100 different contemporary definitions of terrorism. Frequently, the definition depends on one's political goals and objectives, and one's enemies are often labeled terrorists. Governments facing attacks by rebel groups waging unconventional warfare, for example, typically call these groups terrorists as a way to make the rebel group's political demands seem less legitimate. Conversely, viewed from the standpoint of some so-called terrorist groups, governments themselves sometimes appear to be engaged in state-sponsored violence and discrimination against certain populations that could be classified as terrorism. As Laqueur wrote, "Perhaps the only characteristic generally agreed upon is that terrorism always involves violence or the threat of violence."[3]

In the United States, the government has numerous definitions for terrorism. The U.S. Department of Defense definition is, "The unlawful use of violence or threat of violence, often motivated by religious, political, or other ideological beliefs, to instill fear and coerce governments or societies in pursuit of goals that are usually political."[4] The U.S. Central Intelligence Agency (CIA), on the other hand, operates under another definition of terrorism: "premeditated [planned], politically motivated violence perpetrated against noncombatant targets by subnational [not part of a national government] groups or clandestine [secret] agents."[5] However, another agency in the U.S. intelligence network—the U.S. National Counterterrorism

Terrorism is a tactic used by many groups, including white supremacists. As the world changes, different ideologies come into conflict, pushing some people to act out with violence.

A Statement from an Ex-Jihadi

Walid Shoebat is a Palestinian who was once a member of the Palestine Liberation Organization (PLO), a group based in the region of Palestine that has conducted acts of terrorism against the country of Israel, which is the only country in the world where most of the population is Jewish. Shoebat was taught to hate Jews and admitted to committing acts of violence against Israelis. Later in his life, however, he moved to the United States, renounced terrorism, and in 2005, published a book titled *Why I Left Jihad*. In the book, Shoebat explained Islamism, stating,

> *It is no different from the Nazis throwing human beings into ovens. We are witnessing the rise of terror, all over the world, no different from what happened in Nazi Germany ... No one was safe then; no one is safe now ... With Islamism, only those who adhere to militant, radical fundamentalism are safe; the rest of the world are infidels who must be converted or destroyed ... The Jews are not their only target ... The rest of you are infidels, too: Koreans, Japanese, Britons, anyone—even other Muslims who don't adhere to this cult of violence. The motto is "Islam to the world." The earth, they claim, belongs to "Allah and His prophet."*[1]

Jihad is a concept found in the Islamic holy book, the Koran, that advocates fighting against those who do not believe in Islam. It is a teaching that is often translated to mean "holy war." Islamist extremists take this literally, but modern Muslims interpret it to mean an inner struggle against their own doubt or lack of faith. Just as the Bible has passages in it encouraging Christians to fight nonbelievers, which were the basis for the Crusades—a series of holy wars in the Middle Ages—the Koran has several passages about literal warfare, and holy wars that were termed jihads have been waged in the past. Today, non-extremist followers of both Christianity and Islam consider those passages of their holy books to be outdated, and only fundamentalists support killing others in the name of their religion.

1. Walid Shoebat, *Why I Left Jihad*. New York, NY: Top Executive Media, 2005, pp. 14–15.

Center (NCTC), part of the Office of the Director of National Intelligence—uses a slightly different description of terrorist acts: "Premeditated; perpetrated by a subnational or clandestine agent; politically motivated, potentially including religious, philosophical, or culturally symbolic motivations; violent; and perpetrated against a noncombatant target."[6] These are only a few of the different definitions of terrorism used by different parts of the U.S. government.

Gun Show Sales to Terrorists

U.S. residents are 25 times more likely to die by gun violence than residents of other high-income nations. One reason for this is the easy access to firearms. Terrorists know just how simple it is to purchase these weapons in the United States. The ISIS propaganda magazine *Rumiyah* educates readers about the lack of identification requirements for purchasing semiautomatic weapons from private sellers and gun show vendors. In 2017, an article in the magazine stated, "With approximately 5,000 gun shows taking place annually within the United States, the acquisition of firearms becomes a very easy matter."[1]

1. The Editorial Board, "Shunning Gun Control, Helping Terrorists," *New York Times*, June 12, 2017. www.nytimes.com/2017/06/12/opinion/shunning-gun-control-helping-terrorists.html .

The global community of nations has not agreed on a definition either. Members of the United Nations (UN) have not been able to formally adopt a definition, and although several proposals have been offered, none have been accepted. One UN panel defined terrorism as any act "intended to cause death or serious bodily harm to civilians or non-combatants with the purpose of intimidating a population or compelling a government or an international organization to do or abstain from doing any act,"[7] but this definition has not been universally adopted by the UN.

The United Nations Office on Drugs and Crime (UNODC) explained that not having a universal definition is a problem for many reasons, including the fact that "the lack of a definition may facilitate the politicization and misuse of the term 'terrorism' to curb non-terrorist (or sometimes even non-criminal) activities."[8] In other words, without an official definition, a government could potentially call any activity terrorism and punish people who had not even committed a crime at all. Another problem is that it is hard to fight terrorism if officials are not exactly sure what they should be looking for. In October 2005, the representative for the country of Iceland told the UN that "Nations had to come to an agreement on a definition of the term 'terrorism,' for without a consensus of what constituted terrorism, nations could not unite against it."[9] Despite this urging, the UN has still not adopted an official definition as of 2019. In a 2010 article published in the journal *Terrorism and Political Violence*, researchers Leonard Weinberg, Ami Pedahzur, and Sivan Hirsch-Hoefler proposed using or modifying a definition created by researcher Alex Schmid:

> *An anxiety-inspiring method of repeated violent action, employed by (semi-) clandestine individual, group or state actors, for idiosyncratic, criminal or political reasons, whereby—in contrast to assassination—the direct targets of violence are not the main targets. The immediate human victims of violence are generally chosen randomly (targets of opportunity) or selectively (representative or symbolic targets) from a target population, and serve as message generators. Threat- and violence-based communication processes between terrorist (organization), (imperiled) victims, and main targets are used to manipulate the main target (audience(s)), turning it into a target of terror, a target of demands, or a target of attention, depending on whether intimidation, coercion, or propaganda is primarily sought.[10]*

EXTREME ACTS GRAB ATTENTION

"Terrorism has been with us for centuries, and it has always attracted inordinate [excessive] attention because of its dramatic character and its sudden, often wholly unexpected, occurrence."

–Walter Laqueur, historian and political commentator

Walter Laqueur, *The New Terrorism: Fanaticism and the Arms of Mass Destruction*. New York, NY: Oxford University Press, 1999, pp. 3–4.

Weinberg, Pedahzur, and Hirsch-Hoefler explained that Schmid had created this definition by asking various scholars to give him a definition. He received 109 separate definitions, but many of them had common elements. He took 16 of the most commonly mentioned items and combined them into a single definition.

Most definitions, for example, shared the idea that terrorism involves extremely violent acts intended to create fear or terror, often for an ideological, religious, or political purpose. Most terrorism experts also note that terrorists typically use unconventional methods of warfare such as suicide bombing—blowing up a bomb attached to their own body, killing themselves in the

On April 15, 2013, two terrorists detonated two bombs at the Boston Marathon, killing three and severely injuring many others. Their stated reason for the bombings was revenge against the U.S. military presence in Afghanistan and Iraq, but they targeted civilians who had no part in military decisions.

process—and often (but not always) direct their violence against innocent civilians or other people who are not actively fighting rather than the government or organization that they seek to influence.

Experts say a more uniform definition of terrorism would help nations prosecute terrorist actions within their borders and gain cooperation from other nations to fight terrorism on a global scale. As long as nations cannot agree on the definition, each country will use a different legal standard, so nations may have trouble convincing other nations to extradite, or hand over, individuals who have committed terrorist acts for prosecution and punishment.

Revolution

Commentators seem to agree that the reason terrorism is so difficult to define is because it has been applied to many different types of people and to a variety of motives and tactics. As terrorism expert Bruce Hoffman put it, "The most compelling reason [terrorism is hard to define] is because the meaning of the term has changed so frequently over the past two hundred years."[11]

The term "terrorism" was first used during the 1789 French Revolution, and originally, many people did not see it as a bad thing. A peasant rebellion in France against King Louis XVI ushered in a new revolutionary government committed to economic and democratic reforms. The leader of this revolution, Maximilien Robespierre, launched a reign of terror—a campaign that killed between 18,000 and 40,000 people who opposed or were considered a threat to the new government. Executions were conducted publicly using the guillotine, a machine that quickly and efficiently beheaded those condemned as traitors. In this context, terrorism was a tool used to protect the state. As Robespierre explained at the time, "Terror is nothing but justice, prompt [quick], severe and inflexible."[12]

Violent tactics were again used during uprisings in Russia in the late 19th century. A political philosophy known as anarchism arose at this time, advocating the use of violence to overthrow unjust, or unfair, governments. Using a deadly new technology—explosive bombs—a group called the People's Will assassinated Czar Alexander II in 1881 and unleashed a wave of assassinations and bombings throughout the country. Historians say the violent protests eventually helped weaken the cruel czarist system of government in Russia.

The acts of revolutionary terrorism in Russia inspired similar strikes against heads of state and other government targets in countries around the globe. In the 1880s and 1890s, for example, political discontent similar to the anti-czarist sentiment in Russia grew in various parts of the decaying Ottoman Empire—a vast, Turkish-ruled dynasty that covered parts of Asia, Africa, and Europe. In addition, American presidents James Garfield and William McKinley were assassinated during this period, along with two prime ministers of Japan, leaders in India, a French president, an Austrian empress, and a king of Italy.

Abusive Governments

Another type of violence that has been labeled as terrorism by historians involves repression and abuse of power by established governments. This type of terrorism is frequently called state terror. The Russian Revolution, for example, led to the creation of an authoritarian Communist state and to the rise of Joseph Stalin, a leader who implemented a massive campaign of repression and state-run terror designed to eliminate all threats to his rule. During the 1930s, Stalin, through his Great Purge campaign, arrested more than 1.2 million people. About 600,000 ultimately died from torture, execution, or in Russia's inhumane prison system called the gulag.

Also in the 1930s and 1940s, another dictator, Adolf Hitler of Germany, implemented a horrific program to exterminate Jewish people and others he considered to be unworthy of German citizenship. This campaign of state genocide, later known as the Holocaust, is estimated to have killed as many as 11 million people, including about 6 million Jews. State terror was also used by one of Hitler's close allies, Benito Mussolini, a fascist dictator who ruled Italy from 1922 until 1943. Using an armed militia known as the Blackshirts, and later a secret police force, Mussolini eliminated all resistance to his regime and strongly supported Germany's anti-Semitic (anti-Jewish) policies.

Since then, other nations have also used terror to suppress their citizens. In the 1960s and 1970s, for example, Indonesian troops killed, raped, and brutalized thousands of civilians in West Papua and East Timor—regions that were seeking independence from the Indonesian government. Also in the 1970s, the Khmer Rouge regime in Cambodia, led by Pol Pot, became infamous for beating, starving, and torturing an estimated million and a half Cambodians as part of a plan to force the population to work in state labor camps and create a Communist economy.

Terrorists or Freedom Fighters?

One famous historical act of terrorism, according to some people, occurred in Bosnia and helped launch World War I. A group of Bosnian Serb students known as Young Bosnia rose up against the governing Habsburg monarchy, which was centered in Austria and ruled much of Europe. On June 28, 1914, one member of this group, Gavrilo Princip, assassinated the Habsburg archduke Franz Ferdinand and Ferdinand's wife, Sophie. The goal was to break off the southern part of the Austrian Empire to join with neighboring Serbia to form an independent state comprised of Bosnia, Serbia, and other southern Slavic lands. The plan backfired, however, when the Austrian government declared war on Serbia and the growing conflict pulled most of the big powers of Europe into World War I.

Gavrilo Princip is seen as a terrorist by some and a hero by others.

Even today, some people label Princip a freedom fighter instead of a terrorist. In 2014, Sarajevo—the capital city of the country Bosnia and Herzegovina and the place where

Princip carried out his assassination—held a celebration of the 100-year anniversary of the event. Ivo Komšić, the mayor of the city, said, "Under the previous regime we considered him a patriot, all of us who lived in Bosnia ... Franz Ferdinand was a representative of the occupying power. We had Princip's footprints in cement on the pavement where he fired the shot."[13] Café owner Zoran Goljamin felt the same way, saying, "I put [a poster of] Princip up last year when people started saying he was a terrorist ... For me, he's a hero. That's what we learned at school ... Princip was a freedom fighter. His country was under occupation."[14]

Following the end of World War II in 1945, the term "terrorism" was again applied to revolutionary, antigovernment movements—many of them rebellions against European colonial rule. Governments typically called rebel groups terrorists as a form of propaganda, to portray them in a bad light and ignore their demands. Rebel groups, on the other hand, saw themselves as freedom fighters for the cause of political independence or political change. Most groups used the conventional weapons of the age, including machine guns and explosives, and although civilians were sometimes accidentally killed, they targeted mostly government officers and soldiers, causing relatively limited casualties. Rebels justified their use of violence as necessary to acquire freedom and independence from governments that oppressed them.

FREEDOM FIGHTERS?

"The fact that terrorists may claim to be freedom fighters does not mean that we should concede the point to them."

–Louise Richardson, executive dean of the Radcliffe Institute for Advanced Study, a senior lecturer in government at Harvard University, and a lecturer on law at Harvard Law School

Louise Richardson, *What Terrorists Want*. New York, NY: Random House, 2006, p. 7.

During the 1940s, for example, Jewish people who escaped Nazi and European persecution by immigrating to Palestine formed groups, such as the Stern Gang and the Irgun, dedicated to forcing the end of British rule in the region and creating an independent Jewish state. These groups relentlessly attacked British military offices and soldiers stationed in Palestine, and they were repeatedly condemned by government leaders as terrorists. However, these attacks resulted in the creation of the nation of Israel in 1948, and later, two former leaders, Yitzhak Shamir and Menachem Begin, were elected prime ministers of Israel.

Another political rebellion classified as terrorism was the Irish Republican Army's (IRA) guerrilla campaign against British rule in Northern Ireland. An earlier IRA campaign in the 1920s had divided Ireland into two parts—a southern, mostly Catholic region that was granted independence from Britain, and a northern, mostly Protestant district called Ulster, which remained under British control. However, the IRA, together with many Catholics in Ulster, continued to push for a united Ireland that would be wholly independent from British rule. Beginning in the late 1960s, the IRA conducted numerous bombing and assassination attacks. The attacks were aimed primarily at British troops, police officers, prison guards, and judges, but civilians were also frequently in danger, either from direct attacks or stray bullets. After many decades of violence—a period of time known today as "the Troubles"—Northern Ireland was granted self-rule in 1998, a parliament was formed, and the IRA

Today, most of Ireland is an independent country, while Northern Ireland is a self-ruled part of the UK.

agreed to disarm, although it was not until 2007 that the matter was considered mostly settled. Self-rule means that although Northern Ireland is part of the United Kingdom (UK), it has a parliament that decides certain issues for itself, much the way each state in the United States has its own government.

The 1960s brought political terrorism to other regions as well. In Spain, Basque separatists formed the Euskadi Ta Askatasuna (ETA) and demanded independence in response to repression by dictator Francisco Franco. In South Africa, the African National Congress (ANC) and its terrorist arm, Umkhonto we Sizwe (MK, or Spear of the Nation, led by Nelson Mandela), attacked the racist white government and its system of apartheid, or racial segregation, using arson, explosives, and sabotage. In Latin American countries such as Uruguay, Argentina, Brazil, Colombia, Peru, and Venezuela, leftist radicals organized groups that conducted robberies, kidnappings of government officials, and other tactics to undermine governments the rebels viewed as illegitimate and cruel.

The 1960s also saw the beginning of politically motivated Arab terrorism in the Middle East. In 1964, 16 years after the creation of the Jewish nation of Israel amid Arab lands, the Palestine Liberation Organization (PLO) was founded to free Palestinians from what they believed was unjust Israeli occupation. Following the 1967 Arab-Israeli war, during which Israel expanded into several additional Arab territories, PLO leader Yasser Arafat waged a prolonged, bloody terror campaign against Israel. The PLO received financial support from Arab nations such as Libya, a country led by dictator Muammar al-Qaddafi, who, in the 1970s and 1980s, became one of the world's most well-known terrorists. Israel called the Palestinian violence terrorism, but Palestinian terrorists have long viewed themselves as revolutionaries seeking freedom for the Palestinian people. The late Arafat once explained this by saying, "The difference between the revolutionary and the terrorist lies in the reason for which each fights. For whoever stands by a just cause and fights for the freedom and liberation of his land from the invaders, the settlers and the colonists, cannot possibly be called terrorist."[15]

Homegrown Terrorism

Terrorism tactics have also been used by U.S. citizens within the United States. This is called domestic terrorism. In 1892, for example, radical anarchist Emma Goldman conspired with a colleague, Alexander Berkman, to bomb Carnegie Steel Company executive Henry Clay Frick in retaliation for the company's shooting of workers during a strike. In the 1960s and 1970s, the U.S. government itself became the target of left-wing domestic terrorism, this time waged by students. The two most prominent groups were the Black Panther Party, which opposed racial discrimination and oppression and took up arms against the police, and the Weather Underground, which primarily bombed government facilities to protest the United States' involvement in the Vietnam War. Similar attacks were conducted in Europe by groups such as the Red Brigades in Italy and the Red Army

Ecoterrorists: At War to Save the Earth

One form of domestic terrorism is called ecoterrorism. Ecoterrorism is defined by the Federal Bureau of Investigation (FBI) as "the use or threatened use of violence of a criminal nature against innocent victims or property by an environmentally-oriented, subnational group for environmental political reasons, or aimed at an audience beyond the target, often of a symbolic nature."[1] Although ecoterrorists are known to damage property, they generally do not aim their attacks at people.

One of the largest ecoterrorism groups is the Animal Liberation Front (ALF), an animal rights group that has been linked with crimes such as breaking into animal laboratories to release the animals and sabotaging whaling ships. ALF's environmental equivalent is the Earth Liberation Front (ELF), an extremist environmental group that carries out acts of arson (purposely setting fires) against construction that it considers to be damaging to the environment.

1. James F. Jarboe, domestic terrorism section chief, Counterterrorism Division, FBI, Testimony before the House Resources Committee, Subcommittee on Forests and Forest Health, "The Threat of Eco-Terrorism," February 12, 2002. www.fbi.gov/congress/congress02/jarboe021202.htm.

This Oklahoma City memorial was built in honor of the victims of this domestic terror attack.

in Germany—groups that opposed capitalism, imperialism, and colonialism.

The most deadly act of domestic terrorism in U.S. history as of late 2018 occurred on April 19, 1995, when gun enthusiast and former U.S. Army soldier Timothy McVeigh blew up a U.S. government office building in Oklahoma City, Oklahoma. The massive bombing killed 168 people and injured another 853.

In the 21st century, white nationalists—people who believe only white people should live in the United States—have featured largely in the media. They sometimes call themselves the alt-right, or alternative right. (Politically, people to the "right" are more conservative, while people to the "left" are more liberal.) They frequently make violent threats against others, and sometimes those threats are followed through with action. For example, on August 12, 2017, white nationalists held a rally in Charlottesville, Virginia, which was counterprotested by people who did not agree with the white nationalists' views. A 20-year-old from Ohio named James A. Fields Jr. drove a car into the crowd of counterprotesters, killing 32-year-old Heather D. Heyer and injuring 19 others. Jeff Sessions, who was the U.S. attorney general at the time, later stated that the attack fit the legal definition of domestic terrorism.

Not every domestic terrorist is a white nationalist or white supremacist, however. According to Politifact, other groups that have committed acts of domestic terrorism between 2001 and 2016 include "anti-government groups [and] groups with extreme views on abortion, animal rights, the environment or federal ownership of public lands."[16] For instance, the Army of God is classified by the U.S. government as a terrorist organization. This militant Christian group protests abortion by bombing abortion clinics. The Ku Klux Klan (KKK) has not been recognized by the federal government as a terrorist organization, but it is classified this way by the Terrorism Research & Analysis Consortium. The KKK has committed numerous deadly attacks against black, Jewish, LGBT+, and Catholic people since its founding in 1866.

Studies have shown that although Islamist attacks have generally killed more people at once, there have been more attacks by far-right extremists in the United States. It is also important to note that even people who carry out attacks in the name of Islamism are often American citizens or legal residents. According to Albert Ford, an international security researcher, "The terrorist threat in the United States is almost entirely homegrown, as no foreign terrorist organization has successfully directed and orchestrated an attack in the United States since 9/11."[17]

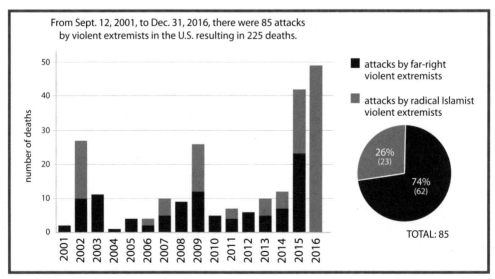

Attacks by radical Islamists are less frequent than those carried out by far-right extremists, but they tend to kill more people at once, as this information from the U.S. Extremist Crime Database shows.

Terrorism in the Late 20th and Early 21st Centuries

Today, the world continues to produce many different forms

of terrorism. Similar to past revolutionary terrorists, some modern-day people use terrorist tactics to achieve political independence and other nationalist goals. After the collapse of the Soviet Union in 1991, for example, an ethnic group called the Chechens (named after where they are from, the Russian republic of Chechnya) waged a struggle for independence. Strikes by both the Russian military and the Chechen separatists killed many civilians. For instance, in 2004, about 1,200 children and adults were taken hostage by armed Chechen rebels at an elementary school in Beslan, Russia. Some hostages were released or escaped, but many others were killed by the Chechens. When the siege ended three days later, more than 330 people—half of whom were children—were dead. In 2009, Russia ended its counterterrorism operation and pulled back the majority of its army, but Chechnya remained part of the Russian Federation.

Because Americans heard about such incidents on the news, many formed the false opinion that all Chechens are violent. This came into play in 2013, when two brothers placed bombs at the Boston Marathon. The Tsarnaev brothers were ethnically Chechen, but they had grown up in Dagestan, which is near but not part of Chechnya, and had lived in the United States legally for years. Some people believed that since the Tsarnaev brothers were Muslim Chechens, their bombing was religiously or politically motivated. However, as CNN pointed out, "Assuming their motives are related to their Chechen origins would be like assuming that Timothy McVeigh's motives were related to his Scottish/Irish origins,"[18] since the Tsarnaevs had lived in the United States for so long.

Other terrorists have motives that seem bizarre to the rest of the

In 1995, a religious cult in Japan released sarin nerve gas in the Tokyo subway, killing 13. Shown here are first responders helping the victims.

world. For instance, in 1995, a Japanese doomsday cult called Aum Shinrikyo carried out Japan's deadliest terror attack to date by boarding five trains and releasing a nerve gas that killed 13 and made 6,000 more sick. In investigating the attack, officials discovered that the cult had previously committed similar crimes. The leader of the cult, Shoko Asahara, "used a mixture of Hinduism, Buddhism, Christianity and yoga to draw followers. They took part in bizarre rituals, such as drinking his bathwater and wearing electrical caps they believed synchronized their brain waves with Asahara's."[19] Asahara's trial spanned eight years, and his testimonies were confusing and difficult to understand; he never explained his reason for the attacks. In July 2018, he was executed.

Examples of state terrorism also exist in the modern world. In the early 1990s, Bosnian Serbs, together with Slobodan Milosevic's regime in Serbia, attacked the non-Serb Muslim population in Bosnia and Herzegovina, an independent republic that once was part of Yugoslavia. Approximately 700,000 people were slaughtered in this campaign, which was euphemistically called "ethnic cleansing." In 1994, another genocide campaign was conducted in Rwanda, a small country in east-central Africa made up of two main social and ethnic groups, Hutus and Tutsis. After a plane carrying the Hutu Rwandan president Juvenal Habyarimana was shot down in April 1994, the presidential guard and other government officials, believing the shooting to be a Tutsi action, approved the killing of Tutsi people

LABELING AN ENEMY

"[Terrorism] is a word ... that is generally applied to one's enemies and opponents, or to those with whom one disagrees and would otherwise prefer to ignore."

–Bruce Hoffman, professor of security studies at Georgetown University's Edmund A. Walsh School of Foreign Service and a recognized expert on terrorism

Bruce Hoffman, *Inside Terrorism*. New York, NY: Columbia University Press, 1998, p. 31.

as well as Hutu people who supported them. In total, about 80,000 people were killed over a period of just three months.

A campaign of state-run terror also developed in the African country of Sudan after an authoritarian, Islamist-Arab government took power in 1989. Sudanese armed forces and government-supported Arab militias known as the Janjaweed attacked the country's black population without mercy. In the region of Darfur, these attacks had killed more than 400,000 people by 2008. Thousands had been raped, and whole villages had been destroyed. More than 2 million people were forced to flee the country. In September of 2016, the Sudanese government launched a chemical weapons attack against its own people in Darfur, killing at least 250.

By far, the terrorism trend that is most frequently in the news, however, is religion-based and centered in the Middle East. Radical Islamists believe Islam has been corrupted by non-fundamentalist influences and have sought to create Islamist states in the region. Although this movement is diverse and made up of many different groups and individuals, it was al-Qaeda—the group responsible for the 9/11 attacks—that brought intense U.S. attention to the problem. Unlike many past terrorist groups, al-Qaeda carried out highly visible suicide attacks that killed as many civilians as possible. Until 9/11, many people in Western society were largely unaware of terrorism. Those who study the issue, however, know that this threat is simply the latest version of a phenomenon that has existed throughout history.

CHAPTER 2

Why Use Terror?

Although politicians and the media often say that terrorists are "crazy," social researchers say otherwise. Studies of terrorist organizations and interviews with individuals who have actively participated in terrorist acts paint a picture of people motivated by either revenge or a desire for justice. They generally know exactly what they are doing, and they have been convinced that their actions are necessary. Most acts of terror are carefully planned and carried out to achieve specific goals. Some are religious or political, while others are ideological, such as those carried out by white supremacists. While there have been a growing number of "lone wolf" attacks carried out by poorly trained individuals with shortsighted objectives, in many cases, members of terrorist organizations have been successful in achieving their desired results. Some have even been elected into leadership positions in government.

Rational Terrorists

The news media loves to cover dramatic events, so terrorist strikes are extensively reported on television and other media outlets. However, this coverage often focuses on the sensational and horrific aspects of the event and portrays terrorists as crazed killers, giving viewers little information or background on the terrorists' objectives. Politicians, too, often respond by calling terrorism evil or suggesting that terrorists have no rational reasons for their violence. Shortly after the 9/11 terrorist attacks, for example, U.S. president George W. Bush stated,

[Terrorists] hate our freedoms—our freedom of religion, our freedom of speech, our freedom to vote and assemble and disagree with each other … These terrorists kill not merely to end lives, but to disrupt and end a way of life … They stand against us, because we stand in their way. We are not deceived by their pretenses to piety. We have seen their kind before. They are the heirs of all the murderous ideologies of the 20th century. By sacrificing human life to serve their radical visions—by abandoning every value except the will to power—they follow in the path of fascism, and Nazism, and totalitarianism.[20]

However, most terrorism experts reject the idea that terrorists are mentally ill or irrational. Dr. Andrew Silke, a United Nations adviser and forensic psychologist at Britain's Leicester University, explained, "The widespread view that terrorists are isolated, vulnerable young men with paranoid or borderline personality disorders is false … Psychologists who have met a terrorist face to face … actually find them to be fairly ordinary."[21] All of the al-Qaeda members studied by Silke came from middle- or upper-class backgrounds, two-thirds were college educated, many had postgraduate degrees, and seven out of ten were married with children.

Reporter Terry McDermott reached the same conclusion. In his book *Perfect Soldiers*, he noted that most of the 19 al-Qaeda terrorists directly responsible for the September 11 attacks on the United States came from "unexceptional backgrounds"[22] that would never suggest the violence that accompanied their deaths. In contrast, other violent criminals such as serial killers tend to have a history of abusing animals and hurting other people before they make their first kill. Mohammed Atta, the pilot of the first plane to hit the World Trade Center, grew up in a middle-class family in Egypt and had done graduate work in architecture. Marwan al-Shehhi, the pilot of the second plane, was a member of the United Arab Emirates army. Hani Hanjour, the pilot of the plane that crashed into the Pentagon, was described as a friendly and polite Saudi who spent a lot of time surfing the internet. Ziad al-Jarrah, the pilot of a fourth plane that crashed in Pennsylvania, was happily married and grew up in a nonreligious, middle-class, westernized Lebanese family. McDermott explained that these men slowly "evolved into devout, pious [deeply religious] young men who, over time, drew deeper and deeper into Islam … [and eventually] saw themselves as soldiers of God."[23] Although they were fully aware that their actions would kill people, they believed it was the right thing to do and that God would reward them in heaven. In their eyes, their actions were just as righteous as donating money to charity or volunteering at a homeless shelter.

USING RELIGION TO JUSTIFY TERROR

"The connection between religion and terrorism is not new. More than two thousand years ago the first acts of what we now describe as 'terrorism' were perpetrated by religious fanatics."

—Bruce Hoffman, professor of security studies at Georgetown University's Edmund A. Walsh School of Foreign Service and a recognized expert on terrorism

Bruce Hoffman, *Inside Terrorism.* New York, NY: Columbia University Press, 1998, p. 88.

People tend to demonize terrorists because they do not want to justify actions that are so horrible and difficult to understand. As terrorism expert Stephen Sloan explained, there is a "public perception … that what the terrorists do is not rational … ascribing [assigning] rationality to an action is viewed as justifying it."[24] The same psychological process often takes place during war, when the enemy is dehumanized in every possible way. In reality, it is possible to understand a person's motivations without agreeing with their actions, and understanding why people perform acts of terror is an important part of stopping attacks from happening in the future. Most experts believe that terrorism is not mindless or done simply for the joy of killing, but rather highly planned and organized violence that is used as a tool to accomplish a larger objective. As Sloan said, "Terrorism is purposeful violence … a means to an end and a way to achieve various goals."[25]

Retaliation and Justice?

The specific goals and motivations for terrorism vary from one individual terrorist to another and among different terrorist groups. At the individual level, experts say, many terrorists are driven by a thirst for revenge for some real or perceived injustice. Terrorism lecturer and author Louise Richardson said conversations with individual terrorists have shown that they often have a very simple, black-and-white view of the world and commit violent acts as vengeance for some suffering they have witnessed within their ethnic, religious, or political group. Richardson explained, "Terrorists see themselves as working heroically for the benefit of others, not for themselves. In this way they see themselves as morally distinguishable from criminals out for their own gain ... They see themselves as defending the weak against the strong and punishing the strong for their violation of all moral codes."[26]

Terrorism expert Bruce Hoffman agrees; he explained that, unlike a common criminal who is motivated by greed or some personal grievance, a terrorist "believes that he is serving a 'good' cause designed to achieve a greater good for a wider constituency [population] . . . [that] the terrorist or his organization purport [claim] to represent."[27] For instance, radical Islamists claim to be acting for the good of all Muslims, even though Muslims do not support or feel they benefit from Islamists' actions.

Sometimes terrorists are radicalized by witnessing, either in person or through television or film, a specific act of injustice. Richardson gave numerous examples of terrorists who have explained how they were "awakened" by the sight or story of atrocities inflicted on innocent people. For example, Vellupillai Prabakharan, the leader of the Sri Lankan Tamil Tigers terrorist group, has said, "It is the plight [trouble] of the Tamil people that compelled me to take up arms ... the ruthless manner in which our people were murdered, massacred, maimed."[28] Richardson also explained that "once a person becomes involved in violence the grievances to be avenged multiply and the opportunities for and means of vengeance expand dramatically."[29] A prime example is the Arab-Israeli conflict, in which the violence on both sides creates a vicious cycle that fuels an endless stream of Palestinians seeking revenge followed by repeated Israeli retaliations.

In other cases, experts suggest, terrorism may be rooted in decades of oppression and poverty, causing deep frustration and hatred of whoever or whatever is believed to be the cause of these issues. Some commentators, for example, believe that the failure of some Middle Eastern nations to provide for their poor, combined with highly oppressive and corrupt leadership in many of these countries, has helped fuel jihadist terrorism. The founder of al-Qaeda, Osama bin Laden, just weeks after 9/11, suggested that this might have been part of his motivation:

> *Here is America struck by God Almighty in one of its vital organs, so that its greatest buildings are destroyed. Grace and gratitude to God. America has been filled with horror from north to south and east to west, and thanks be to God that what America is tasting now is only a copy of what we have tasted. Our Islamic nation has been tasting the same for more than 80 years, humiliation and disgrace, its sons killed and their blood spilled, its sanctities desecrated.*[30]

Many terrorists, therefore, see themselves as victims, not aggressors, and their outrage over what they perceive as deep injustices enables them to commit acts that go far beyond what might be considered justifiable by most people. As Harvard University lecturer and U.S. terrorism expert Jessica Stern has explained, "Because [terrorists] believe their cause is just [fair], and because the population they hope to protect is purportedly so deprived, abused, and helpless, they

Sometimes people join terrorist groups out of a desire to force their government to address the issue of poverty in their country. For example, in this classroom, the government has not provided learning materials or even desks.

persuade themselves that any action—even a heinous [terrible] crime—is justified. They know they are right, not just politically, but morally."[31]

The Social Basis of Terrorist Groups

Up until about 2010, experts say, the majority of terrorist violence was inflicted by organizations rather than individuals acting on their own. Often led by charismatic leaders, these groups recruited people who could easily be convinced that the group's views were right and then increased their recruits' feelings of anger and revenge to create an organized force that could carry out the group's terrorist agenda.

Sometimes the leaders of terrorist groups have higher educations and come from wealthier backgrounds than those recruited as followers. Stern has criticized certain Middle East terrorist groups for actively preying upon the poor and the uneducated to carry out suicide bombing missions. Some Palestinian groups, Stern wrote, fund schools or orphanages for the poor and then recruit young men from these institutions into their terrorist operations. They are viewed as disposable, so the group does not generally care if they get killed, as they can always recruit more from the same place. Many of the jihadist groups, on the other hand, appear to attract more educated and well-off followers and provide them with more intensive and advanced training. For example, psychiatrist and terrorism researcher Marc Sageman looked at 172 members of al-Qaeda and found that two-thirds were middle or upper class, 60 percent had attended college, and many had advanced degrees.

Richardson explained that the most enduring and successful terrorist groups tend to be those with close ties to their communities, whose values and goals are supported by their own societies. In these situations, community members often encourage what they view as an armed struggle for their rights, and in such a society, joining a terrorist group can appear to be one of the noblest actions a young man or woman can take.

Politics versus Religion

Since many terrorist groups tend to identify with complaints about society, a number of experts have concluded that the majority of terrorists are politically motivated. Hoffman, for example, believes that all terrorism is political because it is motivated by a desire to create social change. He explained that violence or the threat of violence is always used as a way to achieve power because terrorists "are unswervingly convinced that only through violence can their cause triumph and their long-term political aims be attained."[32] Ultimately, Hoffman believes, most terrorists seek the power and authority to take specific actions, whether it is the overthrow of a government, a redistribution of wealth, changes in state boundaries, acknowledgement of minority rights, or the establishment of religious rule.

The rise of Islamist fundamentalist terrorism, however, has caused many other scholars to suggest that religion is an equally important part of today's terrorist attacks. Often, these religious terrorists seem to have both religious and political goals—or, putting it another way, political goals that may be driven by religious motives. Sageman, for example, believes that some Muslims, disturbed by the influence of Western culture on the Islamic world, seek essentially religious goals—getting rid of Western and secular (nonreligious) influences, the reestablishment of a fundamentalist version of Islam, and the creation of Islamic governments that will strictly enforce core, conservative Islamic values. While most Muslims with such goals want to use peaceful means to achieve them, there is no denying the existence of a more militant movement.

TACTICS OF THE MARGINALIZED

"Terrorism is not an enemy; it is a method of using violence to gain political objectives. Its tactics are usually employed by weaker, irregular groups against governments that possess organized armies and the modern means for waging war formally and more destructively."

—William Greider, a political journalist and national affairs correspondent for *The Nation*, a progressive magazine

William Greider, "Under the Banner of the 'War' on Terror," *The Nation*, June 21, 2004. www.thenation.com/article/under-banner-war-terror/

Ideally, these jihadists would like to have a large army that could be used to launch a massive military strike against their enemies, but they lack this type of military capacity. Instead, they use terrorism as a way to create fear among secular Muslims and Westerners and motivate them to change government policies.

Despite its lack of military power, this jihadist terror campaign has been one of the most deadly in the history of terrorism. As Hoffman explained, "Terrorism motivated in whole or in part by religious imperatives has often led to more intense acts of violence that have produced considerably higher levels of fatalities than … [those] perpetrated by secular terrorist organizations."[33] In fact, in the last three decades, experts say the most serious and deadly terrorism attacks have all been committed in the name of religion.

Hoffman explained that religious terrorists are often isolated from mainstream society and see themselves as involved in total war that seeks to eliminate anyone who is not a member of the terrorists' religion or religious sect. Because they seek deep fundamental changes in social or political systems, they see no reason to behave reasonably in order to preserve parts of the existing order. Additionally, most religious terrorists also believe strongly in an afterlife, so they often lose their own fear of death. When recruiting, terrorist organizations promise people that their actions will guarantee them a spot in heaven.

Terrorism and Logic

Whatever their motivations, most experts agree that terrorists use terror tactics for purely practical and logical reasons—because they do not have access to conventional military resources or manpower. Moreover, terrorist attacks are a highly effective method of fighting countries or governments that do have massive armies and equipment. Instead of engaging a large army on the battlefield, where they would lose, terrorist groups use different types of warfare tactics such as assassinations, kidnappings, hostage-takings, and suicide bombings as a way to level the playing field.

Terrorist attacks are also relatively cheap, as some bombs can be made mostly with household materials. This makes them affordable for small terrorist organizations with limited budgets. In fact, many commentators have called suicide terrorism the ultimate strategic weapon of the poor since it causes high casualties at such a low cost. Compared to conventional armies, which require billions of dollars' worth of high-tech equipment and personnel, a suicide bombing requires only a willing person, a little training and planning, and a few inexpensive bomb parts. Even the dramatic and complicated 9/11 attacks, according to experts, cost only about $500,000, and a November 2015 ISIS attack on Paris that left 130 dead and hundreds more wounded cost only $10,000, even though it involved bombings and shootings at six different locations in the city.

Terrorist attacks work by generating widespread media publicity—the more spectacular the attack, the greater the media attention it attracts. Bin Laden considered the 9/11 attacks his crowning achievement because of the high shock value, the numbers of people killed, and the symbolism of the targets—the World Trade Center, the center of Western finances and economics, and the Pentagon, the heart of the U.S. military establishment. Modern terrorist groups also like to target civilians, not only because they are easy targets, but because the deaths of civilians typically generate the most outrage and publicity.

Terrorists hope that by creating society-wide fear, they can eventually weaken the will of the government and force political or other surrender. Sometimes, the goal sought is specific, such as the release of imprisoned fellow terrorists. In other cases, the goal is broader and much less direct. The IRA in Northern Ireland,

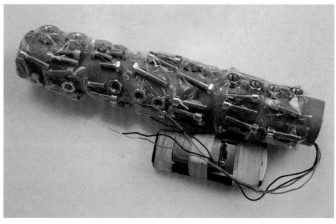

Some bombs, such as this pipe bomb, are very cheap to make but can cause a lot of damage.

for example, sought to make the region chaotic and ungovernable as a way of forcing British police and troops to leave and grant them the right of self-governance. Palestinian attacks on Israel have been designed to make the Israeli occupation of Palestinian territories too expensive in order to force an Israeli retreat and pave the way for the creation of a Palestinian state. Similarly, experts believe al-Qaeda's campaign against the United States was aimed at forcing changes in U.S. foreign policy, such as the withdrawal of troops and a reduced presence in the Middle East.

Is Terrorism Effective?

Some commentators suggest that part of the appeal of terrorism is that it has been successful for some groups, helping them reach political or strategic goals. Some terrorist groups have even acquired political legitimacy and governing power. For instance, most analysts credit suicide attacks performed by the Islamist group Hezbollah with forcing the withdrawal of foreign troops from Lebanon in the early 1980s. These successes, in turn, paved the way for Hezbollah to participate in elections and become a mainstream political party in Lebanon. Terrorist strikes also seem to have helped achieve some of the aims of Palestinian extremist groups such as Hamas, which was successful at derailing peace settlements it viewed as unacceptable. Like Hezbollah, Hamas has converted its terrorist campaign into governing power, winning a majority of seats in the Palestinian parliament in 2006. In 2017, Hamas created a more moderate charter. While continuing to advocate for a free Palestinian state, it no longer calls for the destruction of Israel.

Hezbollah has sent combatants to fight in conflicts in Iraq and Syria. Shown here is a funeral for a Hezbollah member who was killed in one of these battles.

Not All Terrorists Are Muslim

Because Islamist extremists have been so active in the 21st century, many people have begun discriminating against Muslims. However, it is important to remember that not all terrorists are Muslim.

How the word "terrorist" is used—or not used—after an attack plays a role in the stereotyping of people as terrorists. In some cases, there is a good reason for officials not to immediately use the word "terrorist" after an attack. Because the legal definition specifies that an attack must be carried out for political or other gain, the term cannot be applied by law enforcement officials until an investigation reveals the attacker's motives. For example, when a 23-year-old white man carried out several bombings in Austin, Texas, in 2018, he was not labeled a domestic terrorist by the Austin police until the investigation was over. Additionally, domestic terrorism is not a federal crime, so people who are not acting on behalf of a foreign organization such as ISIS tend to be charged with other crimes, such as hate crimes, that do allow them to be prosecuted by a federal court. Because of the severity of most crimes that qualify as domestic terrorism, many people believe the government should reclassify domestic terrorism as a federal crime.

However, the average citizen tends to be unaware of these distinctions in the law, and the media often uses sensationalized language and speculation to create public interest in the story. Occasionally, even law enforcement officials use the term "terrorist" before an investigation is concluded, and many people have accused them of doing it only when the attacker is a person of color. This creates the false impression in many people's minds that only Arab Muslims are terrorists. In fact, according to the Pew Research Center, more U.S. Muslims believe that it is always wrong to kill civilians for political, social, or religious reasons than the general U.S. population. Furthermore, 92 percent of Muslims living in the United States are proud to call themselves American.

Many other terrorist groups, however, have not come close to accomplishing their stated goals. Some commentators, in fact, suggest that nonviolence has been equally or more effective than terrorism in advancing political and humanitarian causes. As Australian professor Brian Martin explained,

> There are many examples where nonviolent action has been effective in situations where violence did not or could not have succeeded. The East Timorese armed struggle against the Indonesian military occupation made little headway over many years … [but] after the liberation movement switched its emphasis from armed struggle in the countryside to nonviolent protest in the cities, it was able to stimulate much greater international support, eventually leading to independence … [Additionally,] in South Africa, armed struggle did little to undermine apartheid [a government policy of racial segregation]. It was only when the challenge to apartheid shifted largely to nonviolent means that great progress was made.[34]

RESPONDING TO ACCUSATIONS

"The notion that the government takes Islamic extremism more seriously than domestic terrorism is, frankly, not true."

—Thomas Brzozowski, counsel to the U.S. Department of Justice on domestic terrorism

Quoted in Ryan J. Reilly, "There's a Good Reason Feds Don't Call White Guys Terrorists, Says DOJ Domestic Terror Chief," *Huffington Post*, January 11, 2018. www.huffingtonpost.com/entry/white-terrorists-domestic-extremists_us_5a550158e4b003133ecceb74

The Lone Wolf

According to political scientist Jeffrey Simon, the biggest terrorist threat of the future may be very different than the terrorist threats of the late 20th and early 21st centuries. In the past, terrorist attacks were almost exclusively carried out by well-organized groups with clear goals. However, since 2010, "lone wolf" attacks have been on the rise. Lone wolf attacks involve one or two individuals—almost exclusively men—who may or may not use the advancement of a cause to rationalize their violence. A lone wolf is often radicalized by propaganda broadcast over the internet, such as on message boards. It is generally after finding an ideology that gives structure to their anger that they pick a scapegoat to attack. For example, a growing movement has centered around the idea of being involuntarily celibate, or unwillingly abstaining from sex. The *New Yorker* explained,

> *In the past few years, a subset of straight men calling themselves "incels" have constructed a violent political ideology around the injustice of young, beautiful women refusing to have sex with them. These men often subscribe to notions of white supremacy. They are, by their own judgment, mostly unattractive and socially inept. (They frequently call themselves "subhuman.") They're also diabolically misogynistic [sexist] ... The idea that this misogyny is the real root of their failures with women does not appear to have occurred to them.*[35]

Many men who end up adopting the incel label are already angry at women and upset about their dating failures when they find online material blaming women for their troubles. Although they structure their grievances around the lack of sex, experts say incels are actually looking for ways to dominate women; as one incel said, "It is obvious that women are inferior, that is why men have always been in control of women."[36] This desire to control women and make them scared to reject men who approach them for sex has led several incels to commit terrorist attacks. For instance, in 2014 in Isla Vista, California, 22-year-old Elliot Rodger "killed six and injured fourteen in an attempt to instigate a 'War on Women'

Elliot Rodger's violent actions made other incels look up to him, but they caused great pain for the loved ones of those who were killed. Shown here is a candlelight vigil for Rodger's victims.

for 'depriving me of sex.' (He then killed himself.)"[37] Rodger's actions made him a hero in the incel community and inspired similar attacks. Several school shootings have also been directed at women who rejected the romantic advances of the shooter, although as of early 2019, none of the school shooters have specifically described themselves as incels.

Lone wolf attacks are hard to stop, in part because lone wolf attackers do not always text or e-mail others about their plans, so there may be no messages for law enforcement to intercept. There are also likely no previously captured co-conspirators or financial transactions that can be traced back to a larger group, which means there is no one who can give authorities information about future planned attacks. Although acting alone seems like it would make a lone wolf terrorist less dangerous, the opposite may actually be true. Simon, who wrote *Lone Wolf Terrorism: Understanding the Growing Threat*, explained:

> Basically the lone wolves are very dangerous and also very creative. There is no group decision-making process, so they are basically free to act upon any scenario they think up. There is no constraint [limit] on the level of violence, because they are not concerned with alienating supporters. Some groups definitely have supporters ... They are difficult to identify and capture working alone. The lone wolves are basically growing in numbers, and in terms of devastation.[38]

While a lone wolf may blog or otherwise publicize his future intentions, law enforcement must wade through enormous amounts of information before deciding what is a credible, or believable, threat and what is simply the empty threats of an online bully with extreme beliefs. Unfortunately, it is sometimes only after an attack that they can be certain. However, lone wolf attacks can benefit larger terrorist organizations. After such an attack, the organization can measure public reaction and claim responsibility if the attack seemingly advances its cause or deny guilt if being associated with the attacker might harm it.

The way the media talks about lone wolf attackers is noticeably different than the way it discusses other terrorists. For instance, on June 17, 2015, a 21-year-old white supremacist

entered a church and murdered nine African American parishio-
ners. At the time, very few media outlets labeled this as a terrorist attack, even though the killer expressed a hatred of people of
color in both an online blog and in a journal he wrote after his
arrest. Much attention was given to his mental health and status
as a social outsider. However, these considerations are rarely
discussed when a mass murderer is a person of color, a citizen
of a foreign country, or an Islamist. Reports of these killers are
much more likely to label them "terrorists" or "thugs." However,
choosing not to label someone a terrorist after they have committed an action that falls within the description of terrorism does
not change the fact that their actions have had a massive effect—
not only on the victims and their loved ones, but on society as
a whole.

The Costs of Terrorism

Acts of terrorism are a cost-effective way for a terrorist organization to wage war, but the cost to society is without a doubt more expensive. In addition to the tragedy of the loss of life and the injuries, the economy is often affected after a terrorist attack. Businesses are often destroyed or closed due to the lack of tourists and local customers, as people tend to stay away from places that have been the site of a recent attack. Police and military budgets inevitably rise after an attack, and this leads to higher taxes. More important still, civil liberties are often sacrificed in the name of safety. Once gone, they are hard to reclaim. These serious costs give many terrorists a reason to continue with their campaigns in the hope that citizens will ask those in power to give in to the terrorists' demands so that life may return to normal.

Death and Injury

The most immediate cost of terrorism is a human one, measured in civilian lives lost and people injured by terrorist attacks. Fortunately, experts say the number of people killed by terrorist attacks around the world has been decreasing. According to Jane's Terrorism and Insurgency Centre, which studies trends in terrorism, the number of worldwide deaths peaked in 2014 at 48,786, but this number dropped dramatically in the following years to 18,475 in 2017. Due to varying definitions of "terrorism," these numbers may not be exactly the same in all reports; for instance, according to the Global Terrorism Database, those numbers are 43,566 and 34,676 respectively. However, the overall trend remains the same: The number of deaths from terrorist attacks is decreasing.

However, it is important to note that the number of deaths and the number of attacks do not always correspond because sometimes one attack kills a large number of people. For

Pulse, a gay nightclub in Orlando, was targeted by Omar Mateen in 2016. Because he claimed support for ISIS, it is counted as a jihadist attack, even though he was not officially part of the group and planned it on his own.

instance, an attack by gunman Omar Mateen on the Pulse nightclub in Orlando, Florida, on June 12, 2016, accounted for 41 percent of all deaths caused by Islamist terrorists between September 12, 2001, and December 31, 2016. Mateen was not part of ISIS, but he claimed that his attack was carried out in support of the organization.

Even when people are not killed, physical and mental injuries occur after terrorist attacks. For instance, interviews with more than 8,000 9/11 survivors, conducted by the U.S. Centers for Disease Control and Prevention (CDC), suggested that more than 43 percent of the respondents suffered some type of physical injury on the day of the attack and more than half of all survivors were still suffering from some type of respiratory problem two years later due to the highly toxic fumes created by the blast. Several years after the attack, thousands of first responders—firefighters, police officers, emergency medical technicians (EMTs), and others who were on the scene to help people—reported serious illnesses, such as cancer and lung disease, caused by breathing in smoke and toxic chemicals.

Another effect of the 9/11 attacks was a rise in mental health issues, including anxiety, depression, and post-traumatic stress disorder (PTSD), a condition in which the patient keeps reliving a highly stressful event. Common symptoms of PTSD include profound sadness or fear; distressing thoughts, feelings, or images of the event; inability to sleep; frightening dreams; and problems with concentration. First responders or bystanders who witnessed the collapse of buildings or the death or injury of others were the most likely candidates for PTSD, but studies have shown that many other people not directly affected by the incident may also have experienced trauma. Children, people with preexisting mental illnesses, or people living near the area of the strike may have feared that they or their families would become victims of a future attack. In fact, the American Psychological Association (APA) Task Force on Resilience in Response to Terror said that even people who simply watched television coverage of the 9/11 attacks reported feeling a high level of stress.

PERCEPTION VERSUS REALITY

"A new trend in terrorism research is to speak about 'homegrown terrorism' as if it were a new phenomenon. However, a review of 'terrorism'—defined most comprehensively as non-state political violence—in the Western world since the French Revolution clearly demonstrates that the vast majority has always been homegrown in the sense that the perpetrators were born, raised, and radicalized in the target country and committed acts of violence for local reasons."

—Marc Sageman, former CIA operations officer and author of the book *Understanding Terror Networks*

Marc Sageman, "'New' Terrorism in the Western World?," *NATO Review*, 2012. www.nato.int/docu/review/2012/Threats-Within/New-Terrorism-Western-World/EN/index.htm

A Damaged Economy

In addition to the trail of deaths and injuries, terrorist events create significant economic damages. Following 9/11, for example, the U.S. Congress created the September 11th Victim Compensation Fund of 2001 to compensate the families of people killed or injured on the day of the attacks. Within three years of the attacks, the fund had distributed $7 billion. Due to the respiratory and mental trauma issues that have come to light in recent years, however, injury costs are expected to increase. Former New York City mayor Michael Bloomberg estimated, for example, that the cost of caring for city workers who became ill as a result of 9/11 would be approximately $393 million a year. In 2011, President Obama signed into law the James Zadroga 9/11 Health and Compensation Act. Over the following five years, $4.2 billion was distributed to first responders who suffered negative health consequences as a result of their service at the attack sites.

Lower Manhattan was covered with ash and dust for weeks after 9/11. First responders who were closest to the site suffered the worst health effects, but the ash floated all over the city and affected the lungs of everyone who breathed it in.

Terrorist attacks also frequently cause property damage. Sometimes this is minimal, such as a bullet hole in a wall; other times, whole buildings are destroyed, as in the 9/11 attacks. Not only were both of the twin towers of the World Trade Center—each with 110 floors—completely destroyed, many other surrounding buildings were either destroyed or seriously damaged. The cost of replacing and restoring these buildings as well as repairing the damage done to public works, infrastructure (such as streets, utilities, and subways), police cars, fire trucks, and ambulances, was incredibly high. According to an August 2002 estimate prepared by economist Robert Looney, "The destruction of physical assets was estimated ... to amount to $14 billion for private businesses, $1.5 billion for state and local government enterprises and $0.7 billion for federal enterprises. Rescue, cleanup, and related costs have been estimated to amount to at least $11 billion for a total direct cost of $27.2 billion."[39] On top of these costs, a number of city businesses were forced to close their doors, and as many as 200,000 people lost their jobs. The tourism industry was particularly affected; during the week after the attacks, hotel occupancy in the city fell below 40 percent, and 3,000 employees were laid off.

The U.S. and world economies also suffered losses. The New York Stock Exchange was closed for six days, and when it reopened, the Dow Jones industrial average (the most widely used stock market indicator) had dropped 684.81 points. Additionally, the entire U.S. air transportation network was shut down for two and a half days, at a loss of $1.5 billion in airfare and cargo shipping fees. In fact, the entire worldwide economy slowed down for about a year. Altogether, 9/11 cost the United States and the world hundreds of billions of dollars in economic losses.

The attacks also had an effect on long-term spending because the U.S. government introduced a series of expensive counterterrorism measures. As a first step, the government spent billions on high-tech equipment to screen for weapons and bombs at airports, harbors, and federal sites. New departments were also created, so money needed to be spent on training employees. One was the Transportation Security Administration (TSA), which was created in November 2001 to screen passengers and their luggage for weapons. Another was the Department of Homeland Security (DHS), whose

Prior to the 9/11 attacks, air travel regulations were much less strict. It is now recommended that passengers arrive for departure several hours before their flight to allow time for passing through security.

main responsibility is to watch for and prevent terrorist threats. Reporter Angie C. Marek noted, "It was the single largest reorganization of the federal government since the creation of the Department of Defense, in 1947."[40]

Since 2001, huge expenditures have been made in the name of homeland security, and the budget seems to grow substantially each year. In 2000, for example, the United States spent only $13 billion on homeland security, but the budget for 2007 was $42.8 billion, an increase of more than 300 percent. The requested budget for 2019 was $47.5 billion. This has created controversy, as many people disagree with some of the ways department money has been allocated and used.

The Most Expensive Fight

Terrorism also sometimes prompts governments to undertake expensive military actions to show that they are protecting national security and taking revenge on the terrorists. Just days after 9/11, for example, President Bush declared a war on terrorism, promising to track down Osama bin Laden and use every resource and tool to disrupt and defeat the terrorism threat. This effort began less than a month later, on October 7, 2001, when the United States attacked Afghanistan's Taliban government, which was accused of harboring al-Qaeda terrorists. In an action that received widespread support from the American public, U.S. troops destroyed al-Qaeda bases in Afghanistan, overthrew the pro-al-Qaeda Taliban government, and ran al-Qaeda leaders out of the country.

In a highly controversial move, the Bush administration

Is the TSA Effective?

Response to the TSA program has been mixed since it was created. In the beginning, many people believed it was necessary to have extra security at airports to prevent terrorists from hijacking more planes, while others were annoyed by the extra time it took to go through airport security. As time has gone on, some people still believe the TSA plays an important role in national security, but more people have shifted to the view that it is unnecessary.

As the website Vox pointed out, "The TSA is hard to evaluate ... Despite some *very* notable cases, airplane hijackings and bombings are quite rare. There aren't that many attempts, and there are even fewer successes."[1] Since the TSA was not catching potential hijackers, no one could tell if this was because no one wanted to hijack a plane in the first place or because the possibility of getting caught and arrested scared people away from trying. To evaluate the TSA, several DHS employees went undercover in 2015 to smuggle fake bombs and weapons through airport security. The TSA failed 95 percent of the tests. According to ABC News, "the review determined that despite spending $540 million for checked baggage screening equipment and another $11 million for training since a previous review in 2009, the TSA failed to make any noticeable improvements in that time."[2]

1. Dylan Matthews, "The TSA Is a Waste of Money That Doesn't Save Lives and Might Actually Cost Them," Vox, September 11, 2016. www.vox.com/2016/5/17/11687014/tsa-against-airport-security.
2. Justin Fishel, Pierre Thomas, Mike Levine, and Jack Date, "Exclusive: Undercover DHS Tests Find Security Failures at US Airports," ABC News, June 1, 2015. abcnews.go.com/US/exclusive-undercover-dhs-tests-find-widespread-security-failures/story?id=31434881.

next expanded the war on terror to invade Iraq, a country that administration officials suggested was linked to al-Qaeda and the 9/11 attacks and which they claimed was trying to develop weapons of mass destruction (chemical, biological, and nuclear weapons that could kill many people at once). On March 19, 2003, U.S. troops invaded Iraq and quickly overthrew the regime of Iraqi leader Saddam Hussein. The war in Iraq, however, was opposed by many people, both in the United States and around the world, because it was viewed as an unnecessary war of choice that had no connection to 9/11. Ultimately, these critics were proven correct when no weapons of mass destruction were ever found and political experts confirmed that Iraq had no involvement in 9/11.

Years after the 2001 attack, trillions of dollars have been spent by the United States for military and reconstruction costs, and thousands of lives have been lost and destroyed. In Afghanistan, for example, more than 2,370 U.S. soldiers were killed and tens of thousands injured. However, the war hit the Afghan people the hardest; reportedly, more than 111,000 Afghan troops and civilians were killed, and even more injured. The war in Iraq is just as grim. As the *New York Times* wrote in August 2018,

> *The war in Iraq, which started in 2003, has resumed and continues in a different form over the border in Syria, where the American military also has settled into a string of ground outposts without articulating a plan or schedule for a way out. The United States has at various times declared success in its many campaigns—in late 2001; in the spring of 2003; in 2008; in the short-lived withdrawal from Iraq late in 2011.*[41]

The financial cost of these ambitious operations has also been high. Since September 11, 2001, in fact, experts say the United States has spent more than $2.4 trillion for military operations, reconstruction, and other programs in Iraq and Afghanistan. As journalist Daniel Trotta reported in 2013, "The U.S. war in Iraq has cost $1.7 trillion with an additional $490 billion in benefits owed to war veterans, expenses that could grow to more than $6 trillion over the next four decades counting interest."[42]

Moreover, many terrorism experts say the military excursion into Iraq has only produced more terrorism. Following the U.S. invasion, an anti-American rebellion developed among Iraqis that soon attracted jihadists from throughout the region. Although the Bush administration denied that the war had increased terrorism and claimed that fighting the jihadists in Iraq prevented them from coming to the United States, the U.S. government's own analysts have contradicted the administration's view. A 2006 National Intelligence Estimate called "Trends in Global Terrorism: Implications for the United States," for example, stated, "The Iraq War has become the 'cause celebre' for jihadists, breeding a deep resentment of US involvement in the Muslim world and cultivating supporters for the global jihadist movement."[43]

Civil Liberties Compromised

Although some people worry about further terrorist attacks, others are more concerned about the threat posed to the individual freedoms and civil liberties that have historically been protected in the world's democracies. In the United States, for example, critics accused the Bush administration of using the war on terror as an excuse to expand the powers of the president and executive branch at the expense of essential democratic freedoms. This criticism was based on several administration initiatives that vastly expanded the government's search, surveillance, and interrogation powers.

Almost immediately after the attacks, for example, Bush proposed new legislation called the USA PATRIOT Act, which is commonly known simply as the Patriot Act. This legislation, the president claimed, was "essential not only to pursuing and punishing terrorists, but also preventing more atrocities in the hands of the evil ones."[44] In the crisis atmosphere following 9/11, Congress passed the legislation quickly and with virtually no debate or opposition. In fact, the bill was introduced and passed by overwhelming majorities in both houses of Congress within just a few days of its introduction. The act was signed into law on October 26, 2001, less than two months after the attacks.

From the start, however, the Patriot Act was highly controversial because it greatly broadened the right of the FBI and police to conduct searches of all Americans' private property and information. Some sections of the act, for example, allowed police to secretly search private homes and property, while others allowed law enforcement to listen to people's phone calls and monitor their internet communications. Still other sections of the new law authorized law enforcement to search a wide variety of personal records, including financial, library,

Typically, for a citizen to be secretly monitored by law enforcement, a judge must sign a warrant after the officers present evidence of why the person is a suspect. The Patriot Act allowed law enforcement to perform these actions without a warrant.

travel, video rental, phone, medical, and church records.

The Patriot Act permitted many of these new searches to be conducted without any type of advance judicial warrant. In some cases, the government was required to obtain a warrant from a special secret court set up under the Foreign Intelligence Surveillance Act (FISA). However, the government generally did not have to show that the person being targeted had committed a crime or even that the person was involved in terrorism, only that the information sought was relevant to a government terrorism investigation. Many searches were also authorized to be conducted in secret, and the law prohibited individuals or businesses affected by certain types of surveillance from ever revealing the fact that they had been asked to provide information to the government. The act even prohibited judicial challenges to most of the government's new powers, giving the FBI virtually unrestrained powers to conduct terrorism investigations.

Civil rights advocates claimed that the Patriot Act threatened individual freedoms that were the basis of American democracy and was an invitation for government abuse of power. Groups such as the American Civil Liberties Union (ACLU) stated that the act allowed FBI agents to investigate American citizens for no real reason and subjected organizations to harassment for protected political activities. The group brought lawsuits claiming the legislation violated Americans' sacred constitutional rights, such as privacy, freedom of speech, freedom from unreasonable searches, and due process. In 2004, a court ruling struck down the FBI's use of National Security Letters (NSLs), which allowed for secret searches of internet and telephone records without a judicial warrant.

Despite the criticism and court challenges, Bush urged that the entire Patriot Act be renewed in 2005 when parts of the law were set to expire. Bush claimed, "The Patriot Act has accomplished exactly what it was designed to do—it has protected American liberty, and saved American lives."[45] After a period of congressional review, the Patriot Act was reauthorized in 2006 with a few safeguards to protect civil liberties. Many people, however, continue to successfully claim that the law is constitutionally flawed. In September 2007, two more federal court decisions on the Patriot Act were issued—the first upholding the 2004 finding on NSLs and the second ruling that two other provisions of the act are unconstitutional because they allow search warrants to be issued without probable cause, as the Fourth Amendment requires. In 2011, despite ongoing opposition to the Patriot Act, Obama signed the PATRIOT Sunsets Extension Act, extending provisions to tap phones, search business records, and conduct surveillance of lone wolves.

HOW DO MOST MUSLIMS FEEL ABOUT ISIS?

"They have nothing to do with Islam … They are distorting Islam. They are exploiting the name of Islam … They are enemies of humankind, enemies of Islam."

– Tahir ul Qadri, Islamic scholar from Pakistan

Quoted in "Islamic Scholar: ISIL 'Enemies of Islam,'" *Al Jazeera*, July 21, 2017. www.aljazeera.com/programmes/upfront/2017/07/islamic-scholar-isil-enemies-islam-170721101325342.html.

The Patriot Act was not the only one of Bush's post-9/11 actions that created civil rights protests. In 2002, he quietly authorized the National Security Agency (NSA)—a secretive government intelligence agency charged with collecting information on foreigners—to spy on certain people inside the United

States without the court search warrants normally required for domestic spying. The president later argued that the program was necessary to rapidly monitor the phone calls of U.S. residents who may have contact with terrorist groups, but critics accused the program of being unconstitutional. Although not everyone is targeted, the idea of the FBI monitoring U.S. citizens has persisted and became the basis of a meme in 2017, with people posting fictional conversations between themselves and the imaginary FBI agent assigned to constantly watch them. In many of these memes, the poster and the agent become friends and exchange advice. While these are generally fun to read, some people have concerns that the memes are making FBI surveillance seem harmless, normal, and even fun. As Chloe Bryan warned on Mashable, "And if the FBI is watching you? It's not because they want to swap book recommendations. There exist genuine concerns about who the FBI chooses to surveil and why."[46]

AMERICANS LOSE FAITH IN THEIR NATION

"[T]he price of this president's military and domestic overreach [since 9/11] has been highest in the loss of faith in America itself, in the values and institutions that have historically defined this nation."

–editorial about the Bush administration's actions, published in the *Los Angeles Times* six years after September 11, 2001

"What We've Lost," *Los Angeles Times*, September 11, 2007. www.stat.cmu.edu/~brian/lost/2007-09-11-la-times.html.

Additional actions taken by the administration in the name of 9/11 included the detention of hundreds of terrorist suspects at the Guantánamo Bay U.S. military base in Cuba without charging them with a crime. The suspects were labeled enemy combatants, a term typically reserved for enemy soldiers captured on a battlefield. The Bush administration also defended certain interrogation techniques—such as waterboarding—in terror investigations that are now classified as torture. Many experts saw these decisions as unconstitutional and a violation of the Geneva Conventions—international treaties that govern the treatment of prisoners of war.

Terrorism and American Immigration

Waterboarding involves pouring water over a person's covered face to make them feel as if they are drowning. Many people consider it to be torture. Shown here is a fake waterboarding that was staged to make people aware of how brutal it is.

The idea of terrorism has had a huge effect on American immigration policy, especially after an investigation into 9/11 revealed that the terrorists had been illegally living in the United States after their student visas expired. In 2003, the DHS created a new division called Immigration and Customs Enforcement (ICE). Many people were—and still are—concerned that terrorists would try to immigrate to the United States and plot attacks from inside the country. According to its website, "ICE was granted a unique combination of civil and criminal authorities to better protect national security and strengthen public safety in response to the deadly attacks perpetrated on 9/11."[47]

Although ICE has had these powers since it was created, they were generally not used to enforce the existing immigration policy until President Obama took office. About 2.9 million people were deported—the most under any president, earning him the nickname "Deporter in Chief."

Most undocumented immigrants were caught at the border between Mexico and the United States. In the past, they had simply been denied entry, but under the Obama administration, they were arrested, held in detention centers until they could have a trial, and then formally deported. Obama's immigration enforcement was controversial because of the amount of money it cost to formally prosecute unauthorized immigrants as well as because of what seemed to be racial profiling happening in immigrant investigations in places other than the border.

During the campaign for the 2016 presidential election, immigration remained a controversial topic. Democrats tend to lean liberally, with many pushing for more open immigration policies, as well as fighting to create a path to citizenship for unauthorized immigrants. Republicans tend to lean conservatively, working to remove as many unauthorized immigrants from the United States as possible. When Republican nominee Donald Trump was elected president, many authorized and unauthorized immigrants worried about their futures.

ICE's raids on places that are believed to be housing undocumented immigrants started with the Obama administration and continued under Trump. Some people believe the raids are necessary to remove suspected terrorists. Others say many of the deportations that have taken place were not justified, claiming that many are deported on technicalities and without regard for individual circumstances. For example, *The Nation* reported that although ICE has been deporting people with a criminal record, most of the crimes were nonviolent and were punishable by either a fine or less than a year in jail. This makes people question whether ICE is truly concentrating on finding terrorists. Critics of ICE are especially concerned about raids that result in families being separated.

Controversy Surrounding Trump Administration Policies

On January 27, 2017, Trump signed an executive order that included a 90-day ban on immigration from certain countries

these critics say, documented immigrants should be protected from deportation by their green card, as has historically been U.S. policy. The DHS argued that the new USCIS policy is necessary because getting such benefits might encourage people to immigrate to the United States. Additionally, L. Francis Cissna, the director of the USCIS, stated, "This policy equips USCIS officers with clear guidance they need and deserve to support the enforcement priorities established by the president, keep our communities safe, and protect the integrity of our immigration system from those seeking to exploit it."[51]

ICE and the DHS have come under fire in recent years as people accuse them of expanding their power and their budget beyond what is necessary, sometimes at the expense of other programs that people feel are more important. For example, when Hurricane Florence was on track to hit several southern states in September 2018, the Trump administration ordered $10 million to be taken from the Federal Emergency Management Agency (FEMA)—an organization that helps citizens who have been affected by natural disasters—and given to ICE. The administration was widely criticized for this move. For instance, Senator Jeff Merkley tweeted on September 11, "As #Hurricane Florence bears down, I discovered today that the Trump Administration is taking money away from @FEMA so that they can pay to put more asylum seekers in detention centers. This is a scandal."[52] Statistics have consistently shown that the greatest threat to any country often comes from within: According to Alex Nowrasteh, an immigration expert at the Cato Institute, the "annual chance of being murdered by somebody other than a foreign-born terrorist was 252.9 times greater than the chance of dying in a terrorist attack committed by a foreign-born terrorist"[53] between 1975 and 2015. Despite all of this, government policies and public fear are still mainly focused on Islamist radicals entering the United States.

CHAPTER 4

Continued Conflict in the Middle East

Most Westerners today probably picture an Islamist suicide bomber of Middle Eastern descent when they hear the word "terrorist." This is not surprising, given that radical Islamist terrorism is the type of terrorism most reported about in Western media. It is the form of terrorism Americans are most familiar with and probably most fearful of.

The modern jihadist movement began in the 1980s in the Middle East and exploded in the new millennium following the U.S. invasion of Iraq. It has now spread around the world, and although most terrorists who have carried out attacks in the United States were not born in a foreign country, some have been influenced by Islamist propaganda. Defeating these jihadists has been the central goal of the U.S. war on terror.

Modern Islamist Fundamentalism

Many modern terrorist attacks, including 9/11, were committed by Islamists. However, Islam is one of the world's major religions, and as terrorism expert and author Louise Richardson reported, "Muslims constitute about a fifth of the world's population."[54] The vast majority of the world's Muslims—members of both the Sunni and the Shia (also spelled Shiite) sects of Islam—are moderate in their views and do not support jihadist terrorism. Most Muslims even see this fundamentalist interpretation of Islam as completely against the true teachings of the religion. Those who believe in terrorist jihad are a minority who follow extremist, fundamentalist versions of the Muslim religion. Terrorism scholars Monte Palmer and Princess Palmer explained, "Jihadists are a self-appointed collection of religious fanatics."[55]

AMERICAN FEAR IS MISPLACED

"Although it remains heretical [unpopular] to say so, the evidence so far suggests that ... the threat presented within the United States by al-Qaeda [has been] greatly exaggerated."

–John Mueller, author and political science professor at Ohio State University

John Mueller, "Is There Still a Terrorist Threat?," *Foreign Affairs*, September/October 2006. www.foreignaffairs.org/20060901facomment85501/john-mueller/is-there-still-aterrorist-threat.html.

Islamist groups remained on the sidelines of mainstream Muslim life for many years. In recent decades, however, fundamentalist Islam has exploded in popularity, and experts say it has inspired today's phenomenon of global Islamist terrorism. Many commentators believe that this growth of radical Islam and jihadist terrorism can be attributed to four contemporary political events.

The first of these events occurred in 1979, when a fundamentalist Islamist revolution led by the Ayatollah Ruhollah Khomeini overthrew the pro-Western shah (or king) of Iran, Mohammad Reza Pahlavi. Khomeini, a Shia religious leader, then openly announced his intention to spread his religious revolution throughout the world, and Iran soon became known as a sponsor of terrorism. The second was the 1982 war in Lebanon that began when Israeli troops occupied southern Lebanon to protect Israel's northern border from Palestinian guerrilla attacks. Terrorist attacks by an Islamist group called Hezbollah were successful in forcing the United States, other foreign troops, and eventually Israel to withdraw from Lebanon. As Richardson put it, the fact that the Americans left the country showed the terrorists "how a superpower can be humiliated by a determined and much weaker adversary prepared to use violence against it."[56]

A third event that helped boost Islamist terrorism was a jihadist war against the Soviet Union in Afghanistan. The Soviets invaded Afghanistan in 1979 in an effort to suppress the spread

The secular government of Iran was overthrown by Islamists led by the Ayatollah Khomeini (center) in 1979. Iran immediately went from being an ally of the United States to being one of its greatest adversaries.

of Iranian Islamism to the nearby Soviet republics of Uzbekistan, Tajikistan, and Turkmenistan. The Soviet presence, however, attracted an army of Islamist militants, called mujahideen. A large number of the mujahideen were funded and trained by Islamist leader Osama bin Laden. For 10 years, these fighters battled the powerful Soviet army, in the process acquiring valuable warfare experience and cementing connections between various jihadist groups. The mujahideen also learned to use sophisticated weapons, many of which were actually supplied by the United States to help defeat the Soviet Union because it was an enemy of the United States at the time. The Soviets were forced to withdraw in 1989, and the lesson learned by Islamist fundamentalists was that they could defeat a superpower militarily. Monte Palmer and Princess Palmer explained, "The jihadists emerged from the war in Afghanistan with an exhilarating sense of victory and an unshakable faith in their ability to reclaim the Islamic world in the name of Allah."[57]

The fourth event that motivated modern Islamist terrorists was the 2003 American invasion of Iraq. After the United States overthrew Saddam Hussein's brutal but secular government, a

AL-QAEDA DID NOT WANT TO INVADE THE UNITED STATES

"[Osama bin Laden] has no interest in attempting to convert Americans or others; he wants the West to remove itself from the Muslim world, broadly defined, so that it can return to the days of the caliphate and the law of Sharia."

–Louise Richardson, executive dean of the Radcliffe Institute for Advanced Study, a senior lecturer in government at Harvard University, and a lecturer on law at Harvard Law School

Quoted in "Islamic Scholar: ISIL 'Enemies of Islam,'" *Al Jazeera*, July 21, 2017. www.aljazeera.com/programmes/upfront/2017/07/islamic-scholar-isil-enemies-islam-170721101325342.html.

power vacuum was left. Jihadists on the run from the war in Afghanistan funneled into the country. Many former citizens of Iraq, believing the U.S. invasion was unfair, took up arms against U.S. troops. Furthermore, established terrorist organizations used the internet to turn people to their cause. Years later, the entire region remains destabilized as a result of the Americans' actions.

Altogether, these political events showed Islamist militants that they could stand up to world superpowers such as the Soviet Union and the United States. Bin Laden became a role model for young, radicalized Muslims, and Islamist fundamentalism began to spread.

The Role of Osama bin Laden

After the Afghanistan war in the 1980s, Osama bin Laden returned to his home country of Saudi Arabia to a hero's welcome. Even the Saudi royal family celebrated his victory over the Soviets. Relations between bin Laden and Saudi leaders broke down, however, following Iraq's invasion of neighboring Kuwait in 1990. Fearful that Iraq would invade Saudi Arabia next, the Saudis turned to the United States for protection and allowed U.S. troops to be stationed on Saudi soil, so bin Laden moved his operations to Sudan. Once there, he joined forces with a

The 9/11 attacks were not meant to signal the beginning of an invasion of the United States. Rather, Osama bin Laden (shown here) had hoped the violence would scare the United States into abandoning its military bases in Saudi Arabia.

Muslim priest, or imam, named Hassan Abdalla al-Turabi, who already had contacts with Khomeini in Iran and who, like bin Laden, wanted to form a global Islamist organization to strengthen Islamic rule in the Middle East.

The global jihadist network became stronger in the 1990s and began launching attacks on U.S. targets. In the first significant attack, on February 26, 1993, a van loaded with explosives was detonated under the World Trade Center in New York City, killing six people and injuring more than 1,000. A second attack happened in Somalia in October 1993. Eighteen U.S. servicemen who were part of a humanitarian mission to that country were killed in a bloody ambush by jihadists. The United States withdrew its forces from Somalia shortly after the attack, and as Monte Palmer and Princess Palmer explained, this "reinforced the jihadist conviction that the United States would withdraw from a country rather than take casualties."[58]

In November 1995, the attacks against the United States continued with the bombing of a Saudi National Guard barracks in Riyadh, Saudi Arabia, killing six Americans. A second attack occurred a few months later, when bombs were detonated in the Khobar Towers, a U.S. Marine facility in Dhahran, Saudi Arabia, killing 19 more Americans. Bin Laden and al-Turabi—and possibly the Iranian government—were believed to be behind these attacks, which experts say were staged to show that Americans stationed in Muslim countries would not be safe, even in their protected facilities.

After the Saudi Arabia attacks, the United States pressured the rulers in Sudan to crack down on al-Turabi. Bin Laden moved his operations to Afghanistan. That country, following the Soviet withdrawal, had fallen into the hands of an Islamist group called the Taliban, which imposed strict Islamic rule. Bin Laden and al-Turabi were financial supporters of the Taliban, and the Afghans agreed to provide bin Laden a refuge. In this secure place, with al-Turabi no longer an active partner, bin Laden organized an international jihadist network that he called al-Qaeda, the Arabic word for "base." Here, bin Laden trained and financed dozens of terrorist fighters and coordinated a series of attacks on the United States.

In August 1998, for example, al-Qaeda used truck bombs to attack U.S. embassies in Nairobi, Kenya, and Dar es Salaam, Tanzania, killing 224 people. In October 2000, al-Qaeda agents bombed the USS *Cole*, but the attack that earned bin Laden the most media attention was 9/11.

The 9/11 attacks marked the beginning of the U.S. war on terror, and terrorist groups continued to attack numerous American and Western targets overseas. In 2002, for example, five attacks were attributed to al-Qaeda, including bombings of a nightclub frequented by tourists in Bali, Indonesia, that killed 202 people. The killing continued for the next several years. In 2005, bombs were set off on three trains and a bus in London, England, killing 52 people, and tourist sites in Bali and Amman, Jordan, were attacked, killing a total of 79 people.

A New Base for al-Qaeda

According to most experts, Iraq became the new center for al-Qaeda terrorism. In fact, after the U.S. invasion of Iraq in 2003, Islamist militants flocked to Iraq to fight U.S. forces just as they came to fight the Soviets in Afghanistan a decade earlier. This branch of al-Qaeda became known as al-Qaeda in Iraq (AQI). The group's goal became sowing sectarian violence—that is, fighting between Iraq's Shia and Sunni Muslims—in order to disrupt U.S. efforts to set up an Iraqi democracy, create instability in the country, and force American troops to go home. As Lionel Beehner of the Council on Foreign Relations explained,

[AQI] aims to topple the ... government in Iraq by attacking Shiites, particularly those who have collaborated with the United States, whether they are civilians, army soldiers, or police officers, primarily in and around Baghdad ... Some of the more radical members of al-Qaeda favor the installment of a caliphate—or Islamic government—in Iraq. Short of that, they seek a safe haven from which al-Qaeda can recruit and train terrorists.[59]

AQI was said to be responsible for countless suicide bomb and improvised explosive device (IED) attacks in Iraq, including a shocking 2006 bombing of the ancient, gold-domed Al Askari mosque in Samarra, Iraq—the third holiest Shia shrine—that sparked a marked increase in the number of Shia-Sunni sectarian attacks. Iraq had become al-Qaeda's training ground, where jihadists learned to become experienced fighters and then returned to wage jihad in their homelands. In 2006, AQI merged with other groups to become ISIS.

The Rise of ISIS

Although U.S. forces defeated the pro-al-Qaeda Taliban government in Afghanistan and removed al-Qaeda operations there, bin Laden was able to escape and establish a new base of operations in a rugged, mountainous region in Pakistan, near the Afghanistan border. There, he was protected from Pakistani troops by local tribal leaders, and the United States was reluctant to invade the area for fear of angering the Pakistani government and the rest of the Muslim world. From this position, bin Laden ran a widespread propaganda campaign that made him the symbol for the global jihadist movement. According to Middle East expert Bruce Reidel, al-Qaeda put out numerous videos and "some 4,500 overtly jihadi Web sites ... [to] disseminate the al-Qaeda leadership's messages."[60] It would take nearly 10 years to capture and kill bin Laden, but this was eventually accomplished in 2011, when President Obama sent a group of highly trained Navy SEALs to bin Laden's base. They burst into his compound and were able to fatally shoot him. For this action, they were hailed as heroes by the American public.

Jihadists continued to expand their operations throughout

the Muslim world and into Europe. One of the most notable signs of this was the July 7, 2005, attack on the London public transport system. Another attack that was carried out in England happened at an Ariana Grande concert in the city of Manchester in 2017. The arena where she was performing was targeted by a suicide bomber, killing 22 people and giving Grande PTSD after the incident. An investigation later revealed that the bomber, 22-year-old Salman Abedi, had a British passport, meaning he was in the country legally. ISIS claimed responsibility for Abedi's attack, but experts could find no proof of a link. One reporter blamed Grande's revealing stage outfits for the attack, saying they were a representation of what Islamists hate about the West, but he received widespread criticism from the public and terrorism experts alike, who noted that Grande and other victims are not responsible for terrorists' actions. When Grande apologized to her fans via Twitter for the fact that her concert was chosen as the target of an attack, thousands responded asking her not to blame herself.

Shown here are the thousands of flowers, balloons, and other items that were left in St. Ann's Square in Manchester in tribute to the victims of the 2017 bombing.

Another European country that has been the target of jihadist attacks is France. On November 13, 2015, terrorists murdered 130 people in and around Paris, France. A majority of

Persecution of Muslims

Fear of Islamist terrorists has caused Muslims around the world to experience persecution. Hate crimes against Muslims in the United States rose sharply in 2001 and again in 2016 after Donald Trump was elected president. Muslims in Paris and London have also been targeted. Even Arabs who are not Muslim have been targeted. In 2018, a Palestinian vlogger named Nas posted a video about the animosity between Jews and Arabs in Jerusalem. As he was filming a video for his Facebook channel, Nas Daily, a Jewish man began chatting with him. When Nas told the man he was Palestinian, the man did not believe it at first, claiming that Nas must be French because he seemed too intelligent to be Arab. When the man's 15-year-old relative joined the conversation, she asked, "Why is he proud of it? ... If it were up to me, I wouldn't let any Arab enter this area ... They want to kill us ... There is no Arab that's not a terrorist."[1] Nas explained to his viewers, "The only people these guys know are the ones on TV: the Arabs trying to kill Jews and Jews trying to kill Arabs. On TV, they don't see ... the majority of people who have no desire for war."[2]

Even if they are not personally targeted for violence, moderate Muslims have been accused of "allowing" their fellow Muslims to be terrorists by not taking a strong enough public stand against terrorism. To show that this is untrue, 19-year-old Heraa Hashmi, an American Muslim college student, compiled a 712-page Google document full of examples of times Muslims have denounced terrorism and other forms of violence, such as domestic abuse, on social media. She used these to create the website Muslims Condemn. Hashmi also noted that accusing Muslims this way means they are "held to a different standard than other minorities: 1.6 billion people are expected to apologise and condemn [terrorism] on behalf of a couple of dozen lunatics ... I don't view the KKK or the Westboro Baptist Church or the Lord's Resistance Army as accurate representations of Christianity. I know that they're on the fringe."[3]

1. "Jews vs. Arabs," Facebook video, 4:12, posted by Nas Daily, February 2, 2018. www.facebook.com/nasdaily/videos/977587759060043/UzpfSTEyNDMzMjQyMDk6MTAyMTc1OTg3MjU2NjAzMTM/.

2. "Jews vs. Arabs," Facebook video, posted by Nas Daily.

3. Quoted in Arwa Mahdawi, "The 712-Page Google Doc That Proves Muslims Do Condemn Terrorism," Guardian, March 26, 2017. www.theguardian.com/world/shortcuts/2017/mar/26/muslims-condemn-terrorism-stats.

them were killed while attending a concert in the Bataclan theater. Firearms as well as explosive suicide vests were used in the killings. The attacks were the deadliest in France since World War II. Several months earlier, 17 had been killed at the office of the satirical magazine *Charlie Hebdo* and a Jewish market in Paris. ISIS claimed responsibility for all of these attacks.

The nation was plunged into a three-month state of emergency. Many civil rights were suspended in an attempt to hunt down other would-be terrorists. In addition, the French military launched a massive attack on Raqqa, Syria, a city out of which ISIS based its operations. However, even after all the bloodshed, France pledged to accept 30,000 Syrian refugees fleeing war and terror in their own nation. French president Francois Hollande stated it was France's "humanitarian duty."[61]

Even though the United States and several European countries have been targeted by terrorists, the majority of attacks take place against Muslims in the Middle East. Experts say attacks on the West represent only 2.5 percent of all attacks each year, but many Westerners are unaware of these trends, since the Western media tends to report only on attacks that happen in Western countries. The Global Terrorism Index creates a ranking of countries that are most affected by terrorism in terms of incidents, damages, deaths, and injuries. In this list, no Western country makes the top 10. In 2016, the 10 countries with the most deaths from terrorism were Iraq, Afghanistan, Syria, Nigeria, Pakistan, Somalia, Turkey, Yemen, Democratic Republic of the Congo, and South Sudan; in Iraq alone, an average of 33 people are killed by terrorists every day.

In April 2014, a Nigerian Islamist terrorist group called Boko Haram gained worldwide attention by kidnapping nearly 280 teenage girls from a local boarding school. The group had been active since at least 2002, but experts have said it may have existed in a less organized form since the late 1990s. Westerners were largely unaware of the group's existence until 2014 because Boko Haram is active only in Nigeria. In a public statement, one of the terrorists said God had commanded him to sell the kidnapped girls into slavery. The hashtag #BringBackOurGirls began trending on social media in response to the kidnapping, and the United States sent troops to Chad, a neighboring country, to help search for the girls.

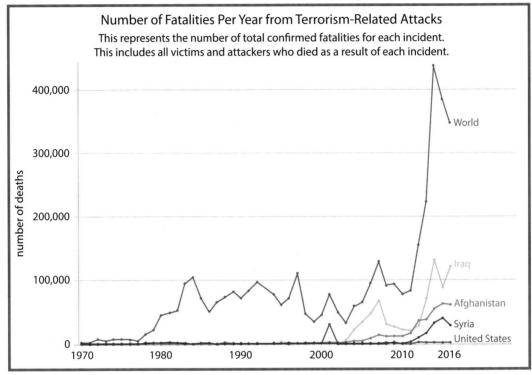

Number of Fatalities Per Year from Terrorism-Related Attacks
This represents the number of total confirmed fatalities for each incident.
This includes all victims and attackers who died as a result of each incident.

Several countries in the Middle East experience far more deadly terrorist attacks each year than the United States does, as this information from the Global Terrorism Database shows.

In the meantime, Boko Haram kidnapped more girls and conducted attacks on multiple towns, causing thousands of deaths and injuries. Although some of the kidnapped girls managed to escape, it was not until 2016 that Boko Haram began freeing some of them during negotiations with the Nigerian government. The United States has considered becoming more involved in opposing Boko Haram, but experts have warned the government that military strength may not be the answer, since their actions are "a direct result of chronic poor governance by Nigeria's federal and state governments, the political marginalization of northeastern Nigeria, and the region's accelerating impoverishment."[62] Instead of fighting, which will lead to the deaths of even more civilians and is not likely to completely eliminate Boko Haram, former U.S. ambassador to Nigeria John Campbell suggested that the United States should work with the Nigerian government to help it address the issues that caused Boko Haram to rise up in the first place. This represents a change in the way the United States has traditionally responded to terrorists.

CHAPTER 5

Moving Forward

A major reason why the United States has historically maintained military bases in Middle Eastern countries is because America relies heavily on oil from those countries to do things such as power cars and heat homes. However, as technology changes and the United States begins to move toward renewable energy from solar and wind power, it must question whether maintaining those bases is worthwhile. Allies in those countries want the United States to stay, but a continued U.S. military presence will leave soldiers as targets of Islamist terrorism. Trillions of dollars have already been spent on military operations and homeland security, and many citizens are beginning to question whether this money would be better spent in other areas, such as improving the U.S. health care system. Others argue that national security is the most important issue. Global trade will continue to consolidate world economies while bringing different belief systems into conflict. While countless organizations continue to work for world peace, there is no shortage of terrorist organizations attempting to gain weapons of mass destruction. If one of these groups were to successfully deploy a chemical, biological, or nuclear weapon, the results could be earth-shattering.

Globalization Brings Terrorists Together

Terrorism has existed for hundreds of years because it has great appeal as a way for the weak and powerless to confront much stronger enemies or powerful governments. For these

An increase in the availability of renewable energy has led to a decrease in the reliance of the United States on foreign oil reserves. Today, rather than protecting oil interests, the U.S. military presence in several Middle Eastern countries is said to be necessary to protect American freedom.

reasons alone, experts say terrorist tactics are likely to continue to be used in the future. While the Pentagon of the United States has elevated possible conflict with the nations of Russia and China as threats to U.S. national security, a growing global jihadist network remains a major concern. Defense secretary Jim Mattis stated in 2018, "We will continue to prosecute the campaign against terrorists, but great power competition—not terrorism—is now the primary focus of U.S. national security."[63]

Today's terrorism is aided by certain developments that are unique to the 21st century. One of the most significant of these forces is globalization—the increased mobility of people and goods throughout the world. Global trade has helped increase development and prosperity, especially in industrialized countries such as the United States. However, although some less-industrialized countries have also benefited, many others have been left out of this prosperity. People in regions still suffering from great poverty and oppression, including many parts of the Muslim world, often feel disenchanted and alienated, and some experts think these conditions create fertile ground for extremist and terrorist groups to grow. In addition, this globalization has fueled a backlash against immigrants to the United States and some European countries.

Improvements in communications that have accompanied globalization have helped increase the ability of terrorists to connect with like-minded supporters and build their terrorist networks. Today, terrorists operating in different countries can communicate, exchange information, rally their supporters, and plan terrorist attacks over the internet. This helps create a global community unrestricted by physical or national boundaries in which participants find their identity in extremist or fundamentalist ideologies rather than in the places where they actually live.

In fact, experts say that the number of websites promoting violence and exalting terrorism has exploded. Gabriel Weimann of Haifa University in Israel stated that websites run by terrorist groups had grown from 12 in 1998 to about 4,800 by 2010. Today, a seemingly limitless number of websites and social media platforms allow would-be terrorists to connect with greater and greater ease. Many of these websites spread radical propaganda in a wide variety of forms. For instance, they may post videos showing terrorists shooting down enemy helicopters with shoulder-fired missiles, bombing vehicles or buildings with improvised explosive devices (IEDs), or shooting enemy troops with assault rifles. By portraying underdog fighters dominating well-equipped military forces, these images are designed to inspire, boost morale, and promote recruitment efforts of terrorist groups. Often, these images are mixed with others that show the death and suffering of poor civilians and their children at the hands of foreign troops—images designed to create feelings of fear, anger, and resentment.

Some websites may actively recruit, but others simply inspire. For example, although Omar Mateen carried out the Pulse nightclub shooting on behalf of ISIS, he was not directly connected to the group in any way. He had learned about Islamist views online and had decided he agreed with them. Mateen is not alone; a 2018 report by New America stated that a total of 49 percent of jihadists had been radicalized online since 2001. According to *NATO Review* magazine,

To the question of how terror networks recruit in the target land, the answer is that they don't. Young people who perpetrate terrorism on behalf of global neo-Jihadi terrorism are mostly self-recruited; they sometimes try to travel abroad to connect with more formal organisations, such as the various al-Qaeda affiliates. They are essentially volunteers who have already decided to join the violent global movement.

If they fail to link up with terrorist organisations, they may still act on their own, on behalf of the violent global movement. Once they have attempted a terrorist act, whether successful or not, they provide a model for other like-minded young people who reject traditional protest and become "copy-cat" actors without any central coordination from a formal conspiratorial organisation.[64]

THE WAR ON TERROR IN IRAQ AND SYRIA

"ISIL is not 'Islamic.' No religion condones the killing of innocents, and the vast majority of ISIL's victims have been Muslim. And ISIL is certainly not a state. It was formerly al-Qaeda's affiliate in Iraq and has taken advantage of sectarian strife and Syria's civil war to gain territory on both sides of the Iraq-Syrian border. It is recognized by no government, nor the people it subjugates. ISIL is a terrorist organization, pure and simple."

–Barack Obama, 44th president of the United States

Barack Obama, "Transcript: President Obama's Speech on Combating ISIS and Terrorism," CNN, September 10, 2014. www.cnn.com/2014/09/10/politics/transcript-obama-syria-isis-speech/index.html

U.S. Involvement in the Middle East

The United States has been involved in various countries in the Middle East since the 20th century, and this continues today, although the motivations have changed somewhat. In the past, the U.S. government claimed that it needed to protect its oil interests as well as search for WMDs. Today, however, the country is involved in wars in multiple countries. For example, in 2017, the United States launched multiple airstrikes in Yemen, Syria, and Iraq. President Trump has vowed that the military will "fight to win,"[65] but experts say this presents difficulties because there is no way to tell what "winning" is. There will be no official surrender from another country, and it will be impossible to know if all of the terrorists have been killed. Even if they have been, more will likely be inspired to take their place.

For this reason, some critics of the government's actions have stated that military strength is not enough; diplomatic relations need to be established with the governments of the targeted countries to help them work out a long-term solution to the terrorists' grievances. They remind people of the way the government in Iraq collapsed soon after the United States overthrew its leader and then left without helping the country establish a new government.

Additionally, critics have noted that focusing on fighting in the Middle East ignores the growing threat of domestic jihadist terrorism. New America reported that of the 15 people who carried out deadly jihadist attacks in the United States since 9/11, all were American citizens or legal residents. Several were born in the United States; most were born into families that had immigrated from places such as Palestine, Afghanistan, and Egypt, but three were African American, two were Russian, and two were white Americans—one born in Texas, the other born in Florida. Some of these terrorists disliked American foreign policy, but others had religious or personal complaints. Experts say that, while determining one clear motivation for terrorism has never been easy, it is becoming increasingly difficult in the era of lone wolf terrorism. However, they are generally motivated by things such as a desire for a sense of purpose combined with Islamist ideology. Many were converted to Islamism after experiencing "personal disappointment, like the death of a parent. For many, joining a jihadist group or carrying out an attack allowed them to become heroes of their own story."[66] Focusing on jihadist groups also ignores terrorist organizations that subscribe to other religions or political ideologies, such as the Army of God or the KKK.

The Weapons of Terrorism

Terrorist attacks are already frequently deadly, but the death toll would increase dramatically if a group or individual could one day gain access to nuclear, biological, or chemical weapons. As terrorism expert Walter Laqueur explained,

> For the first time in history, weapons of enormous destructive power are both readily acquired and harder to track ... Science and technology have made enormous progress, but human nature, alas, has not changed. There is as much fanaticism and madness as there ever was, and there are now very powerful weapons of mass destruction available to the terrorist ... In the near future it will be technologically possible to kill thousands, perhaps hundreds of thousands, not to mention the toll the panic that is likely to ensue may take. In brief, there has been a radical transformation, if not a revolution, in the character of terrorism, a fact we are still reluctant to accept.[67]

Terrorism expert Jessica Stern believes there are several developments that increase the risk that terrorists will use WMDs. First, such weapons are valuable to modern terrorists whose goals include wanting to kill large numbers of people and who appear to be more likely to commit acts of extreme violence. Also, Stern noted that since the breakup of the Soviet Union at the start of the 1990s, WMDs and information about how to use them are readily available in the underground markets. Even some governments, such as the government of North Korea, are believed to be exporting WMD materials for profit. Finally, Stern said, advances in weapons and communications technology have made WMD terrorism easier to carry out.

However, some analysts point out that terrorists may not need to resort to WMDs to carry out attacks. As terrorism experts Daniel Benjamin and Steven Simon explained, the easiest option "is to use 'conventional' means—for the most part, available explosives—to strike targets whose destruction will cause mass casualties and, potentially, far-reaching economic disruption."[68] After all, the 9/11 terrorists used airplanes to create massive destruction. U.S. chemical plants or vehicles that carry chemicals could also be targeted, causing toxic fumes to spread and endanger millions of people. Simple weapons such as pipe bombs and even vans driven at high speed into crowds of people have been used in recent attacks, proving that someone does not need a high-tech weapon to do damage.

One of the most effective weapons used by terrorists is the IED. They are often left hidden on roadsides and used to blow up passing vehicles. Shown here is a U.S. Army unit deliberately exploding IEDs in Afghanistan so no unsuspecting troops or civilians will accidentally set one off and get hurt.

No Clear Solutions

Despite the predictions about the future and the significant resources that have been directed at the problem already, experts remain divided over the best strategies for combating terrorism. To date, various counterterrorism methods have been used with varying rates of success. Before 9/11, for example, many countries saw terrorism as a criminal justice matter and fought it with law enforcement tools. In the United States, the FBI—the investigative arm of the U.S. Department of Justice—was charged with preventing and prosecuting terrorism in the United States. This system prosecuted several major international terrorism cases, including al-Qaeda's 1993 bombing of the World Trade Center. Other defendants were convicted for plotting terrorist attacks that were never carried out.

Cyberterrorism Is Here

The newest form of terrorism, and quite possibly the most difficult to defend against, is cyberterrorism, which could potentially disable a nation's computer systems. Because of rapid technological developments, most industries, businesses, and governments have become entirely dependent on computers and electronic communications. This makes these computer systems highly valued targets. By disrupting these computers through computer viruses, denial of service (DOS) attacks, or other sabotage methods, terrorists could create havoc in key sectors of the economy, such as banking and telecommunications. A cyberattack could shut down vital utilities or air traffic control systems, or even disrupt a country's national defense systems. Hospitals could have their power shut off, traffic lights could be disabled, and sensitive computer files could be stolen. Even without loss of life, daily life could come screeching to a halt. One result of the threat of these types of attacks is that a new in-demand industry called cyber security has been created.

Experts agree the danger of cyberattacks is growing. One notable example was the theft of personal information of nearly 150 million American consumers from Equifax in 2017. Although this was not a terrorist attack, terrorists could benefit from it; for instance, in 2018, Equifax reported that some customers had their passport information stolen, which could be used to make fake passports. Terrorists could also learn from this incident and perpetrate their own similar attack.

After 9/11, however, the United States and some other countries began to see terrorism as more of an international threat. The realization that terrorism is a global phenomenon caused the United States to shift toward a military strategy against al-Qaeda and brought U.S. and some British forces into the bloody conflicts in Afghanistan and Iraq. President Bush consistently argued that U.S. troops must remain in Iraq to prevent the terrorists from attacking Americans at home. After President Obama officially withdrew U.S troops from Iraq on December 18, 2011,

HOW TO WIN A WAR ON TERROR

"Victory will come not when foreign leaders accept certain terms but when political changes erode and ultimately undermine support for the ideology and strategy of those determined to destroy the United States. It will come not when Washington and its allies kill or capture all terrorists or potential terrorists but when the ideology the terrorists espouse is discredited, when their tactics are seen to have failed, and when they come to find more promising paths to the dignity, respect, and opportunities they crave."

–Philip H. Gordon, Mary and David Boies senior fellow in U.S. foreign policy

Philip H. Gordon, "Can the War on Terror Be Won?," Brookings Institute, November 1, 2007. www.brookings.edu/articles/can-the-war-on-terror-be-won/.

the United States returned to the region in 2014 to combat the terrorists of ISIS. As Obama said on June 14, 2016,

Even as we continue to destroy ISIL militarily, we're addressing the larger forces that have allowed these terrorists to gain traction in parts of the world. With regard to Iraq, this means helping Iraqis stabilize liberated communities and promote inclusive governance so ISIL cannot return.[69]

While the situation has since improved, as of late 2018, about 5,000 U.S. troops remain stationed in Iraq to assist and train Iraqi forces.

Supporters of a military approach claim that it has succeeded in preventing another major terrorist attack in the United States by disrupting critical terrorist operations and killing or capturing many senior members of organizations whose skills and experience have not been replaced. As a 2018 article in the *New York Times* noted, "Islamic State attacks in the West fell steeply in 2018 compared with the previous four years … But the number of attempted attacks remained steady, suggesting that the group remains committed to carrying out catastrophic harm."[70] The article stated that in 2016, 14 terrorist attacks were successfully carried out in Europe, but 40 were discovered and stopped before they could happen. Bill Roggio, a senior fellow at the Foundation for Defense of Democracies, credited several factors with this success: "Closer monitoring of social media. Better understanding of the networks. And better coordination with other countries."[71] As of early 2019, ISIS's power also seems to have been greatly decreased; the group no longer controls any cities, and many of its members have been killed or gone into hiding in the desert. However, as ISIS's history has proven, this is not necessarily a permanent situation. As National Public Radio (NPR) noted, "The forerunner of ISIS was al-Qaida in Iraq. The U.S. and its allies dismantled that group a decade ago. The group then re-emerged as ISIS, stronger than ever, as conditions proved more favorable."[72]

How Likely Is a Terrorist Attack?

Despite the fact that terrorism exists, Western citizens do not need to dramatically alter their daily routines out of fear of an attack. The chances of becoming a victim of terrorism remain close to zero in the United States, Canada, and Europe. As political scientist Ben Friedman said, "Conventional wisdom says that none of us are safe from terrorism. The truth is that almost all of us are."[1] News stories about terrorism are much more likely be broadcast and published than stories about less dramatic events, creating the idea that attacks are much more common in the West than they actually are. Each year, Americans have a higher chance of dying from cancer, a car accident, falling out of bed, being struck by lighting, playing football, or choking on food than they do of being killed in a terrorist attack.

1. Ben Friedman, "The Real Cost of Homeland Security," AlterNet, February 9, 2006. www.alternet.org/audits/31514/.

Perhaps the greatest tool for battling terrorism is diplomacy. Political cooperation with allies and compromise between nations can go a long way toward diffusing tensions between different belief systems. In addition, propaganda aimed at discrediting extremism can help win the hearts and minds of those who might be

THE DIFFICULTY OF WAGING WAR AGAINST A TACTIC

"It is far easier to kill a terrorist than to slay an ideology ... As long as the ground is still ripe for insurgency, it's very hard to keep a war ended."

—Gayle Tzemach Lemmon, member of the Council on Foreign Relations

Quoted in Greg Myre, "Where Did the Islamic State Fighters Go?," NPR, January 1, 2018. www.npr.org/sections/parallels/2018/01/01/574967338/where-did-the-islamic-state-fighters-go.

at risk for being radicalized. Just as important is targeting financial institutions that would handle, hide, invest, and disperse assets used to fund terrorist organizations. Weapons cannot be bought and training cannot be paid for without financial resources. In addition, the United States and most other countries continue to dedicate ever-increasing resources to the identification and

Experts say that working with other governments will create more lasting changes than using military force alone. Shown here are U.S. Secretary of State Rex Tillerson (left) and Kuwaiti foreign minister Sheikh Sabah al-Khaled al-Sabah (right) at an international meeting regarding ISIS in February 2018.

surveillance of would-be terrorists. Military action will almost certainly have to remain an option should all other efforts to eliminate terrorist organizations fail.

Most experts agree that there is no single solution for ending terrorism. Instead, a wide variety of strategies will need to be deployed to limit it. A global effort is required. Weapons regularly used by terrorists, as well as WMDs, must be regulated to limit how many are made and who can get their hands on them. Nations need to share information and coordinate operations to catch terrorists before they can carry out their plans. However, since terrorism is a tactic that many groups use rather than one particular group, it may never be fully eliminated. As former FBI director Robert Mueller has stated, "The struggle against terrorism ... may persist for generations."[73]

Introduction: A New Kind of War

1. "Bush Likens War on Terrorism to Cold War," Australian Broadcasting Corporation, May 27, 2006. www.abc.net.au/news/2006-05-28/bush-likens-war-on-terrorism-to-cold-war/1764206.

2. Quoted in William Greider, "Under the Banner of the 'War' on Terror," *The Nation*, June 3, 2004. www.thenation.com/doc/20040621/greider.

Chapter 1: Terrorism as a Concept

3. Walter Laqueur, *The New Terrorism: Fanaticism and the Arms of Mass Destruction*. New York, NY: Oxford University Press, 1999, p. 6.

4. Military Chiefs of Staff, *Department of Defense Dictionary of Military and Associated Terms*, last updated February 15, 2016, p. 241.

5. Title 22 of the U.S. Code, Section 2656f(d). www.cia.gov/news-information/cia-the-war-on-terrorism/terrorism-faqs.html?tab=list-3.

6. "A Chronology of Significant International Terrorism for 2004," National Counterterrorism Center, April 25, 2005, p. vii. www.fas.org/irp/threat/nctc2004.pdf.

7. Quoted in Carroll Payne, "Understanding Terrorism—Definition of Terrorism," *World Conflict Quarterly*, May 2007. www.globalterrorism101.com/UTDefinition.html.

8. "Defining Terrorism," United Nations Office on Drugs and Crime, accessed on October 17, 2018. www.unodc.org/e4j/en/terrorism/module-4/key-issues/defining-terrorism.html.

9. "Agreed Definition of Term 'Terrorism' Said to Be Needed for Consensus on Completing Comprehensive Convention Against It," United Nations press release, October 7, 2005. www.un.org/press/en/2005/gal3276.doc.htm.

10. Quoted in Leonard Weinberg, Ami Pedahzur, and Sivan Hirsch-Hoefler, "The Challenges of Conceptualizing Terrorism," *Terrorism and Political Violence*, vol. 16, no. 4, August 10, 2010, p. 780. www.tandfonline.com/doi/pdf/10.1080/095465590899768.

11. Bruce Hoffman, *Inside Terrorism*. New York, NY: Columbia University Press, 1998, p. 15.

12. Quoted in Hoffman, *Inside Terrorism*, p. 16.

13. Quoted in Charlotte Eagar, "Meet the Assassin Who Sparked World War One," *Newsweek*, June 14, 2014. www.newsweek.com/meet-assassin-who-sparked-world-war-one-254604.

14. Quoted in Eagar, "Meet the Assassin Who Sparked World War One."

15. Quoted in Hoffman, *Inside Terrorism*, p. 26.

16. Miriam Valverde, "A Look at the Data on Domestic Terrorism and Who's Behind It," Politifact, August 16, 2017. www.politifact.com/truth-o-meter/article/2017/aug/16/look-data-domestic-terrorism-and-whos-behind-it/.

17. Quoted in Valverde, "A Look at the Data."

18. Eric Lohr, "What We Know About Chechnya," CNN, April 20, 2013. www.cnn.com/2013/04/20/opinion/lohr-chechnya-dagestan/index.html.

19. Quoted in Scott Neuman, "Japan Executes Cult Leader Responsible for 1995 Sarin Gas Attacks on Tokyo Subway," NPR, July 6, 2018. www.npr.org/2018/07/06/626434965/japan-executes-cult-leader-responsible-for-1995-sarin-gas-attack-on-tokyo-subway.

Chapter 2: Why Use Terror?

20. George W. Bush, "Address to a Joint Session of Congress and the American People," September 20, 2001. www.whitehouse.gov/news/releases/2001/09/20010920-8.html.

21. Quoted in "Wrong to Call Terrorists 'Madmen,'" BBC News, July 9, 2004. news.bbc.co.uk/2/hi/health/3880777.stm.

22. Terry McDermott, *Perfect Soldiers: The 9/11 Hijackers: Who They Were, Why They Did It.* New York, NY: HarperCollins, 2005, p. xvi.

23. McDermott, *Perfect Soldiers*, p. xvi.

24. Stephen Sloan, *Terrorism: The Present Threat in Context.* New York, NY: Berg, 2006, p. 20.

25. Sloan, Terrorism, p. 21.

26. Louise Richardson, *What Terrorists Want: Understanding the Enemy, Containing the Threat.* New York, NY: Random House, 2006, pp. 43–44.

27. Hoffman, *Inside Terrorism*, p. 43.

28. Quoted in Richardson, *What Terrorists Want*, p. 42.

29. Richardson, *What Terrorists Want*, p. 90.

30. Quoted in Richardson, *What Terrorists Want*, p. 43.

31. Jessica Stern, *Terror in the Name of God: Why Religious Militants Kill.* New York, NY: HarperCollins, 2003, p. 282.

32. Hoffman, *Inside Terrorism*, p. 183.

33. Hoffman, *Inside Terrorism*, p. 93.

34. Brian Martin, "Terrorism: Ethics, Effectiveness and Enemies," *Social Alternatives*, 2004, Vol. 23, No. 2, pp. 36–37. www.uow.edu.au/arts/sts/bmartin/pubs/04sa.html.

35. Jia Tolentino, "The Rage of the Incels," *New Yorker*, May 15, 2018. www.newyorker.com/culture/cultural-comment/the-rage-of-the-incels.

36. Quoted in Tolentino, "The Rage of the Incels."

37. Tolentino, "The Rage of the Incels."

38. Quoted in Isaac Chotiner, "A Lone-Wolf Terrorist Is Never Quite Alone," *Slate*, June 13, 2016. www.slate.com/articles/news_and_politics/interrogation/2016/06/why_isis_loves_lone_wolf_terrorists.html.

Chapter 3: The Costs of Terrorism

39. Robert Looney, "Economic Costs to the United States Stemming from the 9/11 Attacks," *Strategic Insights*, August 2002, vol. 1, no. 6. www.ccc.nps.navy.mil/si/aug02/homeland.asp.

40. Angie C. Marek, "Security at Any Price? Homeland Protection Isn't Just Job 1 in Washington; It's More Like a Big Old Government ATM," *US News & World Report*, May 22, 2005. www.usnews.com/usnews/news/articles/050530/30homeland.htm.

41. C. J. Chivers, "War Without End," *New York Times*, August 8, 2018. www.nytimes.com/2018/08/08/magazine/war-afghanistan-iraq-soldiers.html.

42. Daniel Trotta, "Iraq War Costs U.S. More Than $2 Trillion: Study," Reuters, March 14, 2013. www.reuters.com/article/us-iraq-war-anniversary-idUSBRE92D0PG20130314.

43. Director of National Intelligence, "Declassified Key Judgments of the National Intelligence Estimate 'Trends in Global Terrorism: Implications for the United States,'" April 2006. www.dni.gov/press_releases/Declassified_NIE_Key_Judgments.pdf.

44. George W. Bush, "Remarks on Signing the USA Patriot Act of 2001," American Presidency Project, October 26, 2001. www.presidency.ucsb.edu/ws/?pid=63850.

45. George W. Bush, "Speech at the Ohio State Highway Patrol Academy in Columbus, Ohio," June 9, 2005.

www.whitehouse.gov/news/releases/2005/06/20050609-2. html.

46. Chloe Bryan, "The Surprising Poignancy of the 'FBI Agent' Meme," Mashable, February 2, 2018. mashable.com/2018/02/02/fbi-agent-webcam-jokes/#4SnfACC6E5qO.

47. "Celebrating the History of ICE," ICE, last updated December 7, 2017. www.ice.gov/features/history.

48. Julie Hirschfeld Davis and Ron Nixon, "White House Fuels Immigration Debate with Terrorism Statistics," *New York Times*, January 16, 2018. www.nytimes.com/2018/01/16/us/politics/trump-immigration-terror-convictions.html

49. Davis and Nixon, "White House Fuels Immigration Debate."

50. Daniel Shoer Roth, "Even with a Green Card, an Immigrant Can Be Deported Under New Guidelines," *Miami Herald*, July 14, 2018. www.miamiherald.com/news/local/immigration/article214844345.html.

51. Quoted in Roth, "Even with a Green Card."

52. Quoted in Miriam Valverde, "PolitiFact: Yes, Trump Administration Did Transfer $10 Million from FEMA to ICE," *Charleston Gazette-Mail*, September 16, 2018. www.wvgazettemail.com/news/politics/politifact-yes-trump-administration-did-transfer-million-from-fema-to/article_da77a1d1-cbbc-536f-aa06-3f007fbe3a43.html.

53. Quoted in Uri Friedman, "Where America's Terrorists Actually Come From," *The Atlantic*, January 30, 2017. www.theatlantic.com/international/archive/2017/01/trump-immigration-ban-terrorism/514361/.

Chapter 4: Continued Conflict in the Middle East

54. Richardson, *What Terrorists Want*, p. 61.

55. Monte Palmer and Princess Palmer, *At the Heart of Terror: Islam, Jihadists, and America's War on Terrorism.*

New York, NY: Rowman & Littlefield, 2004, p. 1.

56. Richardson, *What Terrorists Want*, p. 65.

57. Palmer and Palmer, *At the Heart of Terror*, p. 99.

58. Palmer and Palmer, *At the Heart of Terror*, p. 117.

59. Lionel Beehner, "Al-Qaeda in Iraq: Resurging or Splintering?," Council on Foreign Relations, July 16, 2007. www.cfr.org/publication/13007/alqaeda_in_iraq.html.

60. Bruce Riedel, "Al Qaeda Strikes Back," *Foreign Affairs*, May/June 2007. www.foreignaffairs.org/20070501faessay86304-p0/bruceriedel/al-qaeda-strikes-back.html.

61. Quoted in Ishaan Tharoor, "France Says It Will Take 30,000 Syrian Refugees, While U.S. Republicans Would Turn Them Away," *Washington Post*, November 18, 2015. www.washingtonpost.com/news/worldviews/wp/2015/11/18/france-says-it-will-take-30000-syrian-refugees-while-u-s-republicans-would-turn-them-away/?noredirect=on&utm_term=.b4c2f56bafd3.

62. Quoted in "U.S. Policy to Counter Nigeria's Boko Haram," Council on Foreign Relations, accessed on September 20, 2018. www.cfr.org/report/us-policy-counter-nigerias-boko-haram.

Chapter 5: Moving Forward

63. Quoted in Helene Cooper, "Military Shifts Focus to Threats by Russia and China, Not Terrorism," *New York Times*, January 19, 2018. www.nytimes.com/2018/01/19/us/politics/military-china-russia-terrorism-focus.html.

64. Marc Sageman, "'New' Terrorism in the Western World?," *NATO Review*, 2012. www.nato.int/docu/review/2012/Threats-Within/New-Terrorism-Western-World/EN/index.htm.

65. Quoted in Ben Hubbard and Michael R. Gordon, "U.S. War Footprint Grows in Middle East, with No Endgame

in Sight," *New York Times*, March 29, 2017. www.nytimes.com/2017/03/29/world/middleeast/us-war-footprint-grows-in-middle-east.html.

66. Quoted in Peter Bergen, Albert Ford, Alyssa Sims, and David Sterman, "Terrorism in America After 9/11," New America, 2018. www.newamerica.org/in-depth/terrorism-in-america/.

67. Laqueur, *The New Terrorism*, p. 4.

68. Daniel Benjamin and Steven Simon, *The Next Attack: The Failure of the War on Terror and a Strategy for Getting It Right*. New York, NY: Times Books, 2005, p. 130.

69. Barack Obama, "Remarks by the President After Counter-ISIL Meeting," White House Office of the Press Secretary, June 14, 2016. obamawhitehouse.archives.gov/the-press-office/2016/06/14/remarks-president-after-counter-isil-meeting.

70. Rukmini Callimachi, "Why a 'Dramatic Dip' in ISIS Attacks in the West Is Scant Comfort," *New York Times*, September 12, 2018. www.nytimes.com/2018/09/12/world/middleeast/isis-attacks.html.

71. Quoted in Callimachi, "Why a 'Dramatic Dip' in ISIS Attacks in the West Is Scant Comfort."

72. Greg Myre, "Where Did the Islamic State Fighters Go?," NPR, January 1, 2018. www.npr.org/sections/parallels/2018/01/01/574967338/where-did-the-islamic-state-fighters-go.

73. Robert S. Mueller III, "Past Event," Council on Foreign Relations, September 28, 2007. www.cfr.org/event/robert-s-mueller-iii.

DISCUSSION QUESTIONS

Chapter 1: Terrorism as a Concept

1. What are some of the common factors in the various definitions of terrorism?

2. Give two examples of violent acts, one from history and one from the modern world. Do you think the people who committed them were terrorists or freedom fighters? Explain your answer.

3. Give an example of domestic terrorism.

Chapter 2: Why Use Terror?

1. Do you believe terrorism is justified if it achieves lasting goals? Explain your answer.

2. Do you agree that all terrorism is political? Why or why not?

3. Give some recent examples of "lone wolf" terrorist attacks.

Chapter 3: The Costs of Terrorism

1. What are some economic costs of terrorism?

2. Do you believe it is worth giving up some civil liberties to make a country safer? Why or why not?

3. Do you believe changing immigration policy is the most effective way to fight terrorism? If so, why? If not, what would you do differently?

Chapter 4: Continued Conflict in the Middle East

1. How did al-Qaeda gain so much power?

2. Do you believe the 2003 American invasion of Iraq was handled well or poorly? What do you believe should have been done differently or kept the same?

3. Give some examples of persecution of Muslims you have heard about in the news or have witnessed yourself. How can you help oppose this persecution?

Chapter 5: Moving Forward

1. Name two possible targets for a cyberattack. How might they be stopped?

2. Name two tools in the war on terror that do not require the use of violence.

3. Do you think a war against terrorism can ever be won? Why or why not?

Cato Institute

1000 Massachusetts Avenue NW

Washington, DC 20001

(202) 842-0200

www.cato.org

> The Cato Institute researches topics such as civil liberties, health care, poverty, and national security. The foreign policy and national security section of its website includes articles about American actions in other countries and ways the United States can deal with or avoid conflict with other countries.

Center for Strategic and International Studies (CSIS)

1616 Rhode Island Avenue NW

Washington, DC 20036

(202) 877-0200

www.csis.org

> The Center for Strategic and International Studies (CSIS) is a nonprofit organization that seeks to advance global security and prosperity by conducting research and analysis and developing policy initiatives for decision makers. One area of focus for CSIS is terrorism, and its website contains a long list of publications on the subject, including reports written by experts, press articles, and congressional testimony.

Council on American-Islamic Relations (CAIR)

453 New Jersey Avenue SE

Washington, DC 20003

(202) 488-0833

www.cair.com

> CAIR's mission is to protect American Muslims and explain what Islam is truly about. The organization advocates for justice, peace, civil rights, and understanding.

Council on Foreign Relations

58 East 68th Street

New York, NY 10065

(212) 434-9400

www.cfr.org

> The Council on Foreign Relations is an independent, nonpartisan membership organization, think tank, and publisher dedicated to being a resource for government, business, and the public on foreign policy issues facing the United States and other countries. Its website offers a wealth of information about the various types of terrorism, terrorist groups worldwide, and the U.S. responses following 9/11.

International Institute for Counter-Terrorism (ICT)

Interdisciplinary Center (IDC) Herzliya

P.O. Box 167

Herzliya 4610101

Israel

www.ict.org.il

> The International Institute for Counter-Terrorism (ICT) is an academic institute and think tank for counterterrorism issues. Its mission is to facilitate international cooperation in the global struggle against terrorism and provide expertise to scholars and governments on terrorism, counterterrorism, homeland security, threat vulnerability and risk assessment, intelligence analysis, national security, and defense policy. Numerous reports are featured on ICT's website, many of them related to Palestinian terrorism.

FOR MORE INFORMATION

Books

Green, Robert. *Cause & Effect: The September 11 Attacks*. San Diego, CA: ReferencePoint Press, Inc., 2015.

> This book examines what happened on September 11, 2001, and how it changed life in the United States.

Grey, Judy Silverstein, and Taylor Baldwin Kiland. *Cyber Technology: Using Computers to Fight Terrorism*. New York, NY: Enslow Publishing, LLC, 2017.

> As technology advances, cyberterrorism is a growing concern. This form of terrorism can be used by organizations, lone wolves, and even foreign governments. The authors discuss what cyberterrorism is and how it can be fought.

January, Brendan. *ISIS: The New Global Face of Terrorism*. Minneapolis, MN: Twenty-First Century Books, 2017.

> Learn more about ISIS, its goals, and how it can be fought.

McCabe, Matthew. *12 Things to Know About Terrorism*. North Mankato, MN: 12-Story Press, 2015.

> This book discusses 12 of the most important things people should know about terrorism.

Websites

Amnesty International
www.amnesty.org/en

> After a terrorist attack, some people find themselves fighting for their rights when their government goes too far in trying to improve security. This organization's website includes news articles about potential human rights violations.

Federal Bureau of Investigation (FBI)
www.fbi.gov/investigate/terrorism

> This part of the FBI's website discusses what terrorism is and how the FBI is fighting it.

U.S. Department of Homeland Security (DHS)
www.dhs.gov/topic/preventing-terrorism

> The main job of the DHS is protecting the United States from terrorism. Its website includes information about ways to prevent terrorism, terrorist weapons, and more.

U.S. Department of State: International Travel
travel.state.gov/content/travel/en/international-travel.html

> This section of the Department of State's website gives travelers tips on how to remain safe while traveling, including staying safe from potential terrorist attacks. The department urges travelers to check its rating of various countries to see whether terrorism is a major problem where someone is thinking of traveling.

"What Teens Can Do Against Terrorism"
troopers.ny.gov/Crime_Prevention/Preparedness/What_Teens_Can_Do_Against_Terrorism/

> This section of the New York State Police website gives young adults tips about how to be prepared in the event of a terrorist attack.

INDEX

PICTURE CREDITS

ABOUT THE AUTHOR

Jason Brainard received a B.A. in anthropology and an M.A. in English from the State University of New York at Fredonia. He studied political violence at the University at Buffalo for two years before ultimately escaping to the beautiful Hudson Valley, where he lives with his wonderful wife and two daughters.